THE
SERPENT TONGUE
LIBER 187

THE SERPENT TONGUE
LIBER 187
Copyright © 2011 Jake Stratton-Kent
Original Cover Art © Stuart Littlejohn
Foreword © Lon Milo DuQuette
All Rights Reserved.

Published in Great Britain by Hadean Press

ISBN 978 1 907881 07 7

OTHER BOOKS BY JAKE STRATTON-KENT

The Book of the Law and its Qaballa. Kiblah 1994
True Grimoire. Scarlet Imprint 2009
Geosophia. Scarlet Imprint 2010

HADEAN PRESS
WWW.HADEANPRESS.COM

THE
SERPENT TONGUE
LIBER 187

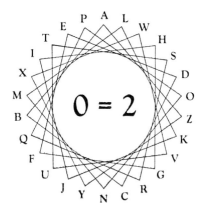

JAKE STRATTON-KENT

CONTENTS

PUBLISHER'S NOTE

THE SERPENT TONGUE: LIBER 187 was first published online in 2000 by Ye Olde Goat's Shoppe and made available for personal use only. With the 2008 reappearance of *The Equinox: British Journal of Thelema* (in whose earlier incarnation much of the writing contained herein first appeared) and subsequent renewed interest in the English Qaballa, permissions were obtained for the publication of a newly revised edition.

The idea that the letters of the alphabet can be equated to numbers, and that meaningful correspondences and values can be attained by way of those numbers, has teased humanity for millennia. Ceremonial magicians appropriated the Hebrew Kabbalah – one of the oldest of such systems – so long ago that to question its use by non-native Hebrew speakers is almost a blasphemy, but question it we do. For some of us, finding meaning in an unfamiliar language has never sat well. Historically the problem was a lack of any other viable system, in particular one devised from the English language. With the discovery of the English Qaballa, that problem was solved.

The subject of an English Qaballa is a controversial one. The idea that a group of English magicians had discovered a solution to the cipher of Chapter 2, Verse 76 of *Liber*

AL: The Book of the Law was met with disbelief and, in some cases, scorn. The fact of its discovery, however, could not be overlooked. As more proofs were revealed and a consistent and coherent system of magick unfolded, the English Qaballa cemented its place in the annals of occult history. *Liber AL*'s puzzle may have no singular solution, and we do not present the English Qaballa as such. All we can claim is that this solution works.

By publishing *The Serpent Tongue* we aim to make public some of the mysteries surrounding the EQ, and to make the system available to any who would follow this arrangement of the English alphabet, wherever it might lead.

We hope you'll find as much value in it as we do.

ALWays,
Hadean Press

Readers will find in this book four spellings of the word 'Qaballa': caballa, kabbalah, qabalah, and qaballa. Briefly, these spellings are defined as follows:

Caballa: the Renaissance adaptation of the Hebrew system.
Kabbalah: the Hebrew system.
Qabalah: the 19th century Hermetic revision of the Christian Cabala.
Qaballa: always refers to the *English Qaballa*.

(See the glossary for more.)

THIS MARVELLOUS STRUCTURE

THERE MAY BE A CERTAIN AMOUNT OF TRUTH IN THE adage *you can't teach an old dog new tricks*, but for this old dog the English Qaballa may very well be the most important new trick I will ever learn.

I suppose I can't be condemned too severely for taking so long to examine this marvellous spiritual instrument. After all, I have spent the better part of my adult life shunning those centres of pestilence who dared discuss or interpret the contents of *Liber AL vel Legis*. I was especially distrustful of the poor souls who, in exchange for a coronation ceremony and the deed to certain real estate in Scotland, were prepared to assume the mantle of spiritual leadership of the world. Indeed, by 1983 my collection of letters from individuals revealing themselves to be the incarnation of Aleister Crowley, or the "one to follow", or "his child & that strangely" or "the child of somebody's bowels", rivalled that of Dr. Regardie. Indeed, shortly before his death the dear man and I even entertained the idea of pooling our letters and communications in a book called *Liber Nutz*.

The authors of nearly every one of these colorful documents claimed to have "cracked the code" of *The Book of the Law* and as proof offered elaborate explanations of the string of numbers and letters (words) that begin the 76th verse of the Second Chapter of *Liber AL vel Legis*:

4 6 3 8 A B K 2 4 a L G M O R 3 Y
X 24 89 R P S T O V A L

For example: the father of one "one to follow" was named Kenneth. The Hebrew word for father being "AB" it was perfectly obvious that ABK referred to his father—whose address at the time of the nativity of his child & that strangely was 4637 GiLMORe ST. But, owing to phenomena arising from the obliquity of the earth's axis between 1904 and the date of his birth, the actual coordinates of his birth were shifted to just across the street at 4638. "What more proof could you want?" He asked. I didn't answer, but I did call Regardie and shared the story. We laughed like schoolyard bullies.

Today I am somewhat ashamed of my arrogant dismissals of what I now see as sincere and poignant pleas for spiritual validation from seekers who were desperately trying far better than I to apply the complex and colorful mythos of Thelema directly to their own lives.

At the time, however, my cynicism hardened with each new revelation and so did my disdain for these still-born prophets with their roaring narcissism, delusions of grandeur, defective Hebrew, disjointed gematria, faulty arithmetic, poor command of the English language, and the utter incapacity to grasp the fact that whoever read their letters would immediately conclude they were mad as hatters.

Like most Thelemites, I did my own share of puttering. In the late 70s I took three yellow legal pads and determined the numeration for each word of *Liber AL*. I did this in a very orthodox manner by treating each English letter as its Hebrew counterpart(s). This was a singularly unsatisfying project. I was perpetually frustrated with uncertainties—uncertainty over whether or not this "t" is Tau or a Teth; or if that "x" is a Tzaddi or a Cheth, or of that "o" is a Vau or an Ayin. Despair followed frustration when my wife, Constance, (who hates the Qabalah) continually pummeled me with the obvious fact that *Liber AL* was not written in Hebrew so why on earth should the letters of its words be translated into Hebrew. My defense was feeble.

"For one reason," I explained to her with sweet condescension, "to see their relationships to significant traditional qabalistic words and concepts."

"And where do those words and concepts come from?" she asked. (She knew the answer. She was just being mean.)

"The Bible... mostly." I mumbled.

"Well, the Bible's not my Holy Book, and *The Book of the Law* doesn't need the Bible to prop it up! Show me a Qabalah in English... one that uses *The Book of the Law* and not the Bible!"

Of course, she was (and is always) right. I eventually abandoned this avenue of research and became, for the most part, contented to appeal exclusively to Crowley's writings for insights and inspiration. As far as exploring the English alphabet—I toyed half-heartedly with *Liber Trigrammaton* the same way a child pushes his broccoli around his plate, but that was it.

I did, however, make one pathetic (yet remarkably successful) foray into *Liber AL*'s practical magick. I projected the numbers and letters from II. 76 upon a kamea of Sol, thusly:

4	6	3	8	A	B
K	2	4		A	L
G	M	O	R	3	Y
X		24		89	
R	P	S	T	O	V
A		L			

I printed it on gold/yellow card stock and laminated it in plastic. Our first test-run of this talisman was to see if it could help us find a new place to live. This may not sound like very serious magick, but if you've ever attempted to find a reasonably inexpensive house to lease in Newport Beach California then I'm afraid you don't really know the meaning of the words "impossible miracle."

Our technique was simplicity itself. We taped the square to the dashboard of our car and drove around the neighborhood where we most desired to live. As rental rates in the new neighborhood were completely out of the price range we could afford, we wisely armed ourselves with a bottle of wine to assure we would not be dissuaded by common sense.

Without going into details (that are fascinating to us, but I'm sure are of little interest to the reader) I will simply report that in the ensuing twenty-five years we have needed to celebrate this ritual six times to locate new homes. It has always worked to the amazement of our neighbors and friends and to our own immense satisfaction.

I mention this magick square not to prove what a clever boy I was or to tout the power inherent in *The Book of the Law*. I bring it up only to point out the rather sad spiritual state into which I had allowed myself to drift. There I was, a hot-shot Thelemite. I militantly preached that *Liber AL vel Legis* was revelatory instrument of the age. I studied it daily and supported that study by performing rituals based upon its deities and formulae; by reading, memorization, and meditation. I was the best damned *Book of the Law* thumper in town! But the most practical thing I had ever done with it was to concoct a crude talisman for house hunting! Hell! Why not just get a sun-bleached buffalo bone, scratch a few markings on it with a sharp stone, and hurl it at the moon?

Well, maybe I'm being a bit hard on myself. The young fool, having neither the wit to see the enormity of his ignorance, nor the good sense to forsake the quest, eventually grew to be an old fool. Don't get me wrong. I don't think I wasted a minute on my magical education. I may have early on abandoned my tinkering with Chapter II, verse 76, but I did spend the next twenty-five years or so immersing myself in the words, images and concepts that form the building-blocks of the magnificent edifice that is Thelema. I speak particularly of the treasures to be found in *Liber AL vel Legis* and the 13 *Holy Books*. What an absolute thrill it is, at this rather late point in my magical life, to finally get a glimpse of what certainly appears to me to be the mathematical mortar that unites these great scriptural stones.

Please do not think that I am presuming to speak for anyone other than myself when I voice my comments in this place. I am not writing as a spokesperson for any of the fine organizations to which I belong, and whose kind forbearance suffer my membership. However, as an individual, I cannot hide my personal enthusiasm concerning the English Qaballa (based upon the ALWHS... etc. progression) and marvellous work being done by Jake Stratton-Kent and others who are continuing to develop and enrich it. They deserve the admiration and thanks of every student of modern magick.

Liber 187 is a particularly brilliant example of how rituals and exercises can be created from this marvellous structure. After I read it for the first time I wrote Jake and told him "It's so clean, it squeaks!" It is indeed so clean it squeaks—English words and phrases relating to other English words and phrases (magick words), familiar words that course through the dynamic matrix of a small collection of spiritual literature that I personally hold sacred.

Perhaps an old dog can learn a new trick or two. I certainly intend to find out.

Lon Milo DuQuette

WHAT WE ALL KNOW ABOUT KABBALAH

> 4. I worship the Devi of all Devis, the great Shri
> Siddha Matrika, whose letters of the alphabet,
> like moonlight, adorn the three worlds. Who is
> the great thread of the letters of the alphabet,
> from which is woven the three worlds, who
> extends from the top of the head to the base
> of the spine. I worship you, O Siddha Matrika.
>
> Vamakeshvara Tantra

MAINSTREAM OCCULTISM, AS EXEMPLIFIED BY THE HOST OF primers appearing year by year, is reluctant to let go of some *neo-traditional* items. By neo-traditional, we of course refer to the notions foisted upon us by the nineteenth century magicians who 'revived' occultism. There are many such notions, and while these may have been expedient in the climate of the Victorian drawing room, it is downright peculiar that they have not been disposed of in today's occult mainstream. Of these notions, the most endemic is the idea that the Kabbalah as a theoretical and practical entity originated wholly within Judaism. In almost any mainstream discussion of the age and provenance of the Hebrew Kabbalah, we find two ideas: one, that the Kabbalah appeared in Jewish communities in the Middle Ages as a full blown system, with a prehistory which the authors leave suitably vague; two, some discussion of the mythical origins of the Kabbalah 'handed down by Angels' to Adam, Moses and so on. Dion Fortune virtually canonised this position with the statement that 'Hebrew is the sacred language of the Western Tradition, as Sanskrit is of the East'. Quite apart from the fact that many of the most important Buddhist scriptures are in Pali, this pernicious myth completely overlooks the importance of Greek and Latin in the (at a decidedly modest estimate) two-thousand-year development of our 'Western' civilisation. Nor does it take into account the extensive base of Sanskrit roots underlying the Indo-European languages of far greater antiquity.

If we examine the writings of the self-assured clergy of the 19th century (such as *A Treatise on the Records of the Creation and on the Moral Attributes of the Creator* by John Bird Sumner, Lord Bishop of Chester) we commonly find them declaiming that Moses must have acquired his doctrine from God because, of those he might have borrowed it from, the Egyptians were superstitious heathens and the Greeks were argumentative and lacked a clear system. Archaeology and a dispassionate reading of history shows that the genius of the Semites and the Greeks was their capacity to absorb ideas and systemise them. Their contacts with great empires with Far Eastern links, as well as their own rich traditions, made this capacity particularly fruitful. No single nation is responsible for the many ideas and techniques found in the Kabbalah or, as we should really refer to this tradition in the period of its original formulation (including the Merkabah mystics), Jewish

Gnosticism. It has accorded with the vested interests of the Church to represent the Old Testament as both superior to (on the grounds of divine inspiration) and distinct from the traditions of other nations. While the Biblical literature does contain many sublime texts and passages, this perception of its superiority and uniqueness is evidently based on religious chauvinism.

These same old-fashioned Christian arguments generally stated that the Jews themselves were incapable, without divine intervention, of originating these same elevated conceptions of deity themselves. Indeed, many an anti-Jewish pogrom of the past was mounted on the pretext of the Jews' evident unworthiness to hold ideas vaguely akin to those of the Christians!

Crowley, arguably the most important of the nineteenth century revivalists, was at pains to disperse such myths. Of his innumerable contributions to modern occultism, among the more important was undoubtedly his attempt to re-establish the 'Greek Qabalah' in modern magical studies. The Grecian influences on the Hebrew Kabbalah are so extensive that it is astonishing that the mainstream can still fall between the two schools of medieval versus mythical origins of the Hebrew system.

The almost grudging admission of Greek gematria into the post-revivalist canon is – absurdly – as second fiddle rather than grand original. Only the influence of the 'crusty old myth of Hebrew as the original language' prevents this from being seen perfectly clearly in the historical materials. The resistance to the English Qaballa is of the same kind. So dominant is this outworn thinking that gematria conversions from *The Book of*

the Law are routinely compared with fragments of the
Jewish scriptures. It is difficult to see what good could
come of comparing concepts derived from *The Book of
the Law* – no matter into what alphabet one converts
them for gematria purposes – with Hebrew scripture.
Indeed, it is entirely alien to Kabbalistic method to do
so. If you insist upon using Hebrew or Greek gematria to
interpret *AL*, the proper course would consist of taking
a given word or phrase, converting it into Greek or
Hebrew characters, and then seeking another word or
phrase within *AL* (or at least *The Holy Books of Thelema*)
which had the same value in the alphabet selected.
Yet virtually all the material in both *Liber D* and *Liber
MCCLXIV* (Crowley's Hebrew and Greek qabalistic
dictionaries) is derived from non-Thelemic sources.

It is an astonishing fact that despite traditionalist
assertions that the Jewish 'qabalah' stands on firmer
ground, there is no Qabalistic dictionary of *AL* available
in Hebrew (or Greek) as there is with English. There is
far more English Qaballistic data available than either
Hebrew or Greek, and it is derived from the Thelemic
texts themselves, permitting gematria comparisons
to be done entirely within the text, as it is meant to
be. Qaballistic exegesis provides a symbolic language
via central texts that thus serve as an incredibly
sophisticated mystical model and a nigh inexhaustible
storehouse of magical materials in a variety of forms
as discussed elsewhere in this book. English Qaballa's
capacity to provide us with such a tool is inestimably
greater than reliance on systems only indirectly related
to our tradition and symbols. To return to the point, the
real origins of the Hebrew system are extremely simple

to determine – and the truth must out. It is not a new truth, academically speaking, but it is taking so long to percolate out into the mainstream that it needs clearly setting forth in a more concise and collated form than the scattered references in several of the thickest books on the old hands' bookshelves.

Now, while there is no doubt that the medieval Kabbalah contains or reflects themes from extremely ancient sources from many disparate cultures (from the occultist's perspective, one of the worst features of the Renaissance Christian Cabbala was its removal of the pagan elements from the Hebrew system), equally there is no doubt that the various elements which constitute the medieval Kabbalah possess an underlying unity. This unity must derive from an earlier culture which sought to unify the wisdom traditions of many cultures into one. Any candidate for the role must be a tolerant and sophisticated culture, with a vested interest in racial and religious equality. Such a culture is not to be found among the Jews themselves, nor originally in the Roman Empire, nor – despite the medieval origin of (the term) Kabbalah – could it safely be sought in Spain, despite the tolerance of the Moslem rulers of the day. The only such cultures are the Hellenistic world resulting from the conquest of the Persian Empire by Alexander the Great, and the Persian Empire itself, particularly under Cyrus the Great.

Here we shall restrict ourselves to the former, about which a great deal more is currently known. In particular, we should examine the most tangible symbol of this cultural synthesis, the Great Library of Alexandria. Two-fifths of the population of Alexandria were Jews, and they greatly outnumbered those living in Jerusalem. The language of these Jews was not Hebrew, but Greek. Among the most famed of their scholars was Philo of Alexandria. Philo's 'writings are a defence of Jewish myths and prophetic utterances, interpreted allegorically, in terms... of Hellenistic theology... in the language of the current cultured Alexandrian religio-philosophy of his day.' (G.R.S. Mead, *Thrice Greatest Hermes*, V.1, p.139.)

Philo was not the first to do this, simply the best known. It is, ultimately, idle to distinguish between the Neoplatonist, Gnostic and Pythagorean influences upon Kabbalah as if they were separate themes; in fact the distinction between Alexandrian Neoplatonism and Gnosticism is extremely difficult to draw, while Plato was strongly linked to the school of Pythagoras. The main point is, these ideas were all part of the Alexandrian world picture and – for occultists at least – Kabbalah without these influences would hardly exist as a separate topic.

'The coming of the Greeks had other than political consequences for Judaism. Hitherto Jews and Greeks had known little of one another; now they were brought into the closest contact. One after another on all sides of Judah there sprang up centres of Greek culture, by all of which, but especially Antioch and Alexandria, the Jews were greatly influenced. Not only did they engage in trade with these cities, but encouraged by both Ptolemies and Seleucids who offered them rights of citizenship, and attracted by the greater freedom of Greek life, they went and lived in them. There they adopted Greek habits and customs and even Greek names; they read Greek literature and studied Greek philosophy. Most important of all, they learnt the Greek language, employing it originally in trade and social intercourse, but afterwards for purposes of religion. Quite early they began to translate the O[ld] T[estament] into Greek – first the Pentateuch, which was completed by 250 [BC], and then gradually the remainder of the sacred books... the complete hellenicisation of Judaism, which must at one time have seemed likely... was providentially checked by the Maccabean revolt; but we must never underestimate the importance of this period of intercourse between Jews and Greeks...' (Peake's *Commentary on the Bible*. p62. 1952 edition.)

Given this absurd preference for Judeo-Christian texts for gematria values, the fondness for Biblical forms and the refusal to depart from Fortune's 'Christian' theory of the qabalah, it is very important to remind ourselves who exactly the Neoplatonists were.

Neoplatonism, incidentally, was founded in Alexandria. The Neoplatonists were the last and greatest opponents of Christianity in the Roman world, whose goal was a synthesis of the wisdom of the ancient nations, unified by Greek thought. This goal was very nearly achieved in their own day, and with the rediscovery of the Hermetic literature in the Renaissance it was very nearly achieved again, but for the utmost exertions of the Church to oppose it. It is ironic, then, that the attempts of the Jews to correlate this noble system with their religion culminated in the efforts of 'Christian Cabbalists' to convert Jews to Christianity!

The first translation of the Hebrew scriptures into Greek in 250 BC, the first of a long line of such translations, was accomplished under the patronage of the second of the Ptolemies, who greatly increased the size of the Library founded by his father. It is upon this king's coins also that we first find the Greek alphabet used as numbers, a century before the Jews were to follow suit. When the Jews made the change, it was upon the instigation of the Maccabean kings, anxious to reassert Hebrew culture after their wars with the Seleucids. From this point on, the Jewish mystical tradition strives to depart from the Gnostic miscellany which preceded it; the attempt to retain purely Jewish forms only became possible with the collapse of the Hellenistic world, after a period of three centuries – the length, for convenience in this book, of the Ptolemaic dynasty.

It was during this Hellenistic phase that the cross-cultural elements of Judaic mysticism first gained much of their present shape. The Hebrews may well have had prior contact with several of the cultures whose themes are resumed in the Gnostic syncretic period, but the form in which the Kabbalah retains these themes, and the spirit in which it interprets them, is Hellenistic. For example, our seven planetary spheres may well derive from a Sumerian model, entering Jewish tradition via the Babylonian captivity. But it is the later Gnostic form, with the seven archons and the ascent of the soul through the spheres, that has determined the manner in which the Merkabah tradition retains this theme.

Whether the Hebrews introduced it to the Greeks or vice versa is irrelevant; the form in which it survives is shaped by Greek thought, even if the thinker may have been a Hellenised Jew, or a Syrian or an Indian. Of whatever nationality, intellectually he was a citizen not of Jerusalem but of Alexandria, the language of his tradition not Hebrew but Greek. The same is true, after all, of the various Gnostic movements of which the Merkabah tradition is representative.

Alexander brought Buddhist India into the tradition we so glibly describe as 'Western'. Buddhist ambassadors dwelt in the kingdoms of the Ptolemies and Seleucids, and Buddhist ideas are among the strongest influences upon Gnosticism. But it is Buddhism through the eyes of a citizen of the Hellenic world, and the same is undoubtedly true of the Semitic elements of our Gnostic heritage. Medieval Kabbalism can only be seen as a late Jewish reworking of the ideas which shaped Gnosticism and Neoplatonism. Despite the important role the Jews played in Alexandrian culture, their religion was reinterpreted along with the others; this was inevitable since the only intellectual tradition in a position to synthesise the world's religions, including Judaism, was Hellenistic philosophy.

The evidence of the Greek and Hebrew use of letters as numbers on coins is not the end of the story. Some form of gematria in both languages can be traced further back, although some old Hebrew texts may conceivably have been altered for gematria purposes at some later date. However, the antiquity of numerical, magical and cult ideas in connection with both alphabets is considerable, and no final conclusions can presently be drawn from the existing evidence. Influences within the Persian Empire (including both Egyptian and Indian territory) upon both Greek and Hebrew culture are established and extensive before the Alexandrian period. This must be the subject of a later study.

Philo, and indeed many another Jewish writer of the Hellenistic era, has been seen as an apologist for his culture, endeavouring to revamp its 'primitive' conception of God, Creation and so on in terms of the more advanced and transcendent Greek philosophy. If the models and mathematical ideas embodied in Kabbalah had a pre-Hellenistic form, it was not to be found among the Jews, but among the great civilisations of Egypt, Persia and India and their predecessors whom the Hellenistic culture had absorbed.

All these influences were to emerge in various forms in the various Gnostic schools of the period (approximately 300 BC to AD 250). One of these Gnostic schools, quite probably based in Jerusalem but competing with many other Jewish and non-Jewish Gnostic sects, was the Merkabah mystics. Scholem, the greatest Jewish scholar of our day, distinguishes these mystics from the Kabbalists, a medieval European phenomenon inspired by the *Book Bahir* which possesses many traces of this earlier tradition, and may have been preserved by some Jewish community in the region of the Black Sea. Still later, as this new tradition flowered in Medieval Spain, the Kabbalists were to consciously readopt the themes of Neoplatonism which had been current in Alexandria.

The Merkabah mystics are responsible for the *Hekhaloth* books. These 'Chariot mystics' are generally confused with the much later Kabbalists, who retained many of their ideas. As Scholem says in his *Origins of the Kaballah*: 'Kabbalah... not only claimed to be the legitimate successor of... the Merkabah but also pretended to represent their actual content in their own teachings.'

Scholem has also shown that the whole conception of these chariot saints – many of whom were highly placed in the hierarchy of the Jerusalem Temple – was derived lock, stock and barrel from the Gnostics. The Gnostic theme of rising through the seven planetary spheres, under the presidency of hostile Archons, is precisely reproduced by their Seven Palaces. He also points out that this school is not concerned particularly with the interpretation of the Old Testament.

In other words, we are talking about a mystical technique within Jewish Gnosticism, rather than the 'Literal Kabbalah' or the use of the number/letter equivalencies of Gematria. (If one thing is certain from the history of Kabbalah it is that Gematria is far older than the system often erroneously believed to have originated it.) However this may be, it is evident that this practical technique bears considerable resemblance to magical techniques nowadays considered Kabbalistic. We should note, then, that this 'rising on the planes' – a mystical approach the origin of which is still much disputed – is not delivered to us by the Hebrew system but through it.

Hebrew godnames proliferate on many so-called Gnostic gems, but nearly always in Greek characters. It is significant too that the elements which the Kabbalah borrowed from the Alexandrian period are those most useful to occultists. As an example, take the Tables of Correspondences, *à la Liber 777*, which Fortune ridiculously claimed constituted the 'Oral Tradition' formerly concealed but revealed by Mathers and Crowley. The 'Doctrine of Correspondences' is a

Neoplatonist concept, and its place in present day Western occultism derives from the Renaissance synthesis, not a concealed Talmudic school.

Furthermore, Scholem notes: 'The fact that the original Merkabah mystics in Palestine prescribed the use of specific Greek formula for certain occasions deserves special attention.' Indeed, many of the Names of Power, etc. which appear, like so many Gnostic pass-words, in these texts are Hebraicised Greek, i.e., bastardised Greek terms written in Hebrew characters.

So it was that 'Greek thought mingled with Hebrew thought, particularly in Alexandria... Jewish Gnosticism absorbed ideas such as the Neo-Platonic theory of creation by emanations, the ten spheres and four levels of the Pythagorean tetraktys, the Four Elements of Empedocles, and the Ptolemaic system of astrology; and among a host of other schools, arose that of the Qabalists.' (Kieren Barry, 'A Brief History of Gematria', supplement to *Liber MCCLXIV*.) Yet these ideas are today seen all too often as a uniquely Hebraic contribution to the Western Tradition. Note, Kieren does not speak of Kabbalists, but of Jewish Gnostics; this author is painstakingly accurate and not afraid to blow away the sacred cows of a tradition supposedly practising the Method of Science.

While such themes are central to the whole system of Qabalah, their involvement with the Hebrew language is entirely secondary. It is a little known fact that Mathers plagiarised the entire introduction to *The Kabbalah Unveiled* from a distinguished scholar, C.D. Ginsburg. Since the introduction, rather than the garbled fragments of *The Zohar*, is what is chiefly useful in the book, I advise students to demand Ginsburg's instead. Therein they can read: 'Nothing can be more evident than that the cardinal and distinct tenets of the Kabbalah in its original form... are derived from Neo-Platonism. Any doubt upon this subject must be relinquished when the two systems are compared. The very expression *En Soph* which the Kabbalah uses to designate the Incomprehensible One, is foreign, and is evidently an imitation of the Greek [APEIROS]... R. Azariel, whose work, as we have seen, is the first Kabbalistic production, candidly tells us that in viewing the Deity as purely negative, and divesting him of all attributes, he followed the opinion of the [Greek] philosophers.'

It is significant, too, that the word *gematria* is of Greek origin. Gematria means 'geometry', not word association. The so-called 'Greek Qabalah' sought numbers that were significant in geometrical terms, in terms of divine proportions, an idea which was to greatly influence the architects of the Gothic cathedrals. In the Greek scriptures (including, but not restricted to, the New Testament) we find that nearly every important name or term has properties which make sense in terms of such canons of proportion; these may, as Sterling says in his enormously influential *Canon*, derive from the artistic canons of the Egyptians, or at least from Graeco-Egyptian reinterpretations of them. It is important to realise the role of Egypt as an influence upon Greek thought, since virtually every major Greek sage is said to have studied there, and the centre of the Hellenistic world after Alexander was Alexandria in Egypt. Not only was Neoplatonism founded in Alexandria, but nearly every major Greek philosopher is said to have 'sojourned in Egypt' (much like the infant Christ in fact!) or learned from one who had.

The place of Egyptian gods in modern occultism has been erroneously attributed to the Egyptology craze current at the founding of the Golden Dawn. That should be The Hermetic Order of the Golden Dawn – Thrice Greatest Hermes, to be precise – a Greek conception of Tahuti, whose voluminous writings are still referred to as the *Book(s) of Thoth*; some indeed are listed in Crowley's resumé of Greek sacred texts. The Graeco-Egyptian element of our tradition is not derived from the 1800s, or even 1904. On the contrary, this influence can be traced, at the very least, to the period three to four hundred years BC with the founding of the Ptolemaic dynasty in Egypt. The revitalised Egyptian tradition was transplanted wholesale into Europe by the Romans; the cult of Isis, revived by Ptolemy I with the aid of the Egyptian priest Manetho and an unnamed initiate of the Greek Eleusian mysteries, was the most popular in Italy before the official adoption of Christianity.

The Western Tradition of magick in the modern period owes its survival to the revival of the Hermetic tradition in the Renaissance, when Neoplatonist ideas once again nearly toppled the Church. It is fitting here to mention the great Renaissance magus Giordano Bruno, described affectionately by Frances Yates as a Hermetic 'extremist' whose enthusiasm for the Hermetic books extended to 'taking Renaissance magic back to its pagan source, abandoning the feeble efforts of Ficino to do a little harmless magic whilst disguising its main source… utterly flouting the religious Hermeticists who tried to have a Christian Hermeticism... proclaiming himself a full Egyptian who, like Celsus... deplores the destruction by the Christians of the worship of the natural gods of Greece, and of the religion of the Egyptians, through which they approached the divine ideas [the Aeons or Archetypes] the intelligible Sun, the One of Neoplatonism'. The resurgence of Graeco-Egyptian elements in Western occultism is due to their all-pervading presence within that tradition.

What is surprising is not that those elements persist, since without them the tradition would scarcely exist, but that the Hebrew elements should have persisted alongside them, since for any but academic and comparative purposes they are inessential, obscurantist, and do much to reinforce the effects of previous religious conditioning which initiation is intended to remove.

It is evident that no central element of Qabalah as employed by Western occultists is specifically Judaic in origin. As Bonner notes: 'Greek presents fewer difficulties for western students. We are more familiar with its symbols, and its structure is closer to English than is Hebrew. Also the fact that it is written from left to right and uses vowels, unlike the north-western Semitic languages, makes it an altogether less intimidating proposition'.

The special pleading for the retention of Hebrew as uniquely special and suitable in modern magic has thus taken three hammer blows. Firstly, the outdated idea that Hebrew represents the primal language from which all others are descended – a key idea in its status in the past – has been rightly dismissed by Umberto Eco as 'a 'crusty old myth'. His terse phrase is too concise and to the point to resist retaining in polemics in future! Secondly, the idea that it is the first sacred language of the West has to contend with the antiquity of Sanskrit and its even more ancient predecessor, both of which lay in back of major Western language groups and are undoubtedly sacred tongues. Lastly even the apparently axiomatic historical primacy of its alphabet is doubtful. Proto-Sinaitic, the ancestor of Phoenician and Hebrew, though described as an alphabet, more closely resembles a syllabary; its lack of characters for vowels is continued in Hebrew, making Greek the first true alphabet as such.

Since all this is so, we can see the relationship of English to the Greek alphabet, its close relationship to that other magical alphabet, Runic, and its descent from the pre-Sanskrit mother-tongue in a completely different light. In this Light – that of a forward-looking Qaballistic Renaissance – our own language attains its overdue apotheosis.

PART ONE

Given the linguistic, religious and cultural distance between Hebrew Kabbalists and Thelemic magicians, the gravest difficulties existed in accessing or even understanding these elements of Kabbalistic practice. This at least was the case before the discovery of the English Qaballa in November 1976.

– from *Liber 187*

PRESENTING THE QABALLA OF *AL*

A	L	W	H	S	D	O	Z	K	V	G	R	C
1	2	3	4	5	6	7	8	9	10	11	12	13

N	Y	J	U	F	Q	B	M	X	I	T	E	P
14	15	16	17	18	19	20	21	22	23	24	25	26

THE ENGLISH QABALLA INVOLVES MANY COMPLEX AND sophisticated structures and leads to many important correlations of ideas. These matters also can be left largely for magical experiment rather than intellectual discussion. Accordingly this book deals with hands-on applications which will enable the magician to explore its complexities for themselves, and provide them with a qaballistic framework capable of almost infinite diversification as they require.

The English Qaballa (EQ) is a qabalah and not a system of numerology. A qabalah is distinguished by three qualities: a specific language; a 'holy' text or texts; and mathematical laws at work in them. Fuller's descriptions of 'what a qabalah is' have been published in *The Equinox: British Journal of Thelema*. Suffice it to say for now that the language in question is English and the texts the Class A or *Holy Books of Thelema*, particularly *The Book of the Law* otherwise known as *Liber AL* or simply *AL*.

The appearance of the English Qaballa is specifically predicted in *Liber AL*, and certain conditions, clues and even frameworks are delineated, none of which had been satisfactorily dealt with until the discovery of EQ. It was above all necessary that such a key should make sense of Chapter II verse 76 – two enigmatic lines of 'numbers and words':

'4 6 3 8 A B K 2 4 A L G M O R 3 Y X 24 89 R P S T O V A L. What meaneth this, o prophet? Thou knowest not; nor shalt thou know ever. There cometh one to follow thee: he shall expound it.'

When I first had my attention drawn to the existence of a purported English Qaballa, my first reaction as a Qabalist was to use it on this meaningless string of digits and characters. I converted all the letters into their numerical equivalents in the English Qaballa, and added them to the numbers in the series.

4 6 3 8 A B K 2 4 A L G M O R 3 Y = 129
 4 6 3 8 1 20 9 2 4 1 2 11 21 7 12 3 15

X 24 89 R P S T O V A L =222
22 24 89 12 26 5 24 7 10 1 2

129 + 222 = 351

The numbers 129 and 222 bear interesting qualities for a qabalist. However, I was not studying a manuscript copy but a printed text, which did not separate the series into two lines as in the original; consequently I simply added up the total of both lines at that time and obtained the number 351. This number is the sum of the numbers 1 to 26, and naturally the sum of the numbers attributed to the letters in English Qaballa.

Since that time I have frequently studied this cipher in the manuscript version of *Liber AL* and have obtained a mental picture of it, consisting of two lines as it appears in the original. There are seventeen numbers and letters in the first line and eleven in the second (both significant numbers) but in the manuscript the 'x' at the beginning of line two suggested to me that I calculate 17 by 11, obtaining 187 – the numerical value of the phrase ENGLISH ALPHABET.

Which brings me to Chapter II verse 55, another key verse of *Liber AL* in which that phrase occurs:

'Thou shalt obtain the Order & Value of the English Alphabet; thou shalt find new symbols to attribute them unto.'

This is a strange verse containing ambiguity and apparent faults in grammar. What is meant by 'them'? 'English Alphabet' is a single whole; the text does not say 'the letters of the English Alphabet' (or does it?). So 'them' must refer to the 'Order & Value'.

This is interesting as a Qaballistic 'in-joke', because the phrase ORDER & VALUE = 117 = LETTERS; so in fact the sentence can be read: 'Thou shalt obtain the <letters> of the English Alphabet; thou shalt find new symbols to attribute them unto'.

Jokes like that can unhinge a man after a while. This is not funny, because in the 93 Current 'there ain't no Sanity Clause'; there is however a 'prodigal son' or 'bad fairy' clause, and the front contender for this role is undoubtedly Austin Osman Spare, the prodigal son of the 93 Current.

AOS, as we shall refer to him, discovered independently of Crowley that the English Alphabet is possessed of all the qualities of a hieratic language – a language used by priests and magicians for their holy books and rituals because it possesses qabalistic and magical virtue. AOS used the English Alphabet in various ways. He found 'new symbols' which constituted his 'Alphabet of Anon'; he combined the original characters (A,B,C, a, b, c, etc.) into sigils; and among other things he reversed and jumbled syllables and words to obtain spoken spells – all of the things practical qabalists and magicians have done with earlier hieratic languages such as Sanskrit, Hebrew, Arabic, Coptic and Greek.

AOS, as a result, was one of the first to prove *The Book of the Law* literally correct in its claims concerning the magical virtue of the English Alphabet. He did not deal with its qabalistic virtues except in terms of the Practical Qabalah. But then he *was* a prodigal son! Those were in any case the earliest days of our not-so-new-now Aeon. Now we have become a tradition rather than a revolution, and that is a good thing; occultists function better as preservers and developers.

In fact, the 93 Current is so well preserved that in some areas development seems almost heretical. Nevertheless, the English Qaballa is a development, over twenty years old and acid resistant, water-tight and possessed of enough potency to stop the most determined qabalist in his tracks, exclaiming,

'EUREKA! Someone's found it!' All known methods of the so-called 'Literal Kabbalah' can be applied to the Class A texts with English Qaballa, particularly Gematria, but also Notariqon, Temurah and 'Mystic' numbers (being the sum of the integers from 1 to a significant number, inclusive, usually in the two digit range; for instance 351 is the 'mystic' number of the English Alphabet/26). Theosophic Addition (the practice of adding all the digits of a number together, as 21 = 2 + 1 = 3, thus interrelating the symbolism of these two numbers, and reducing composite numbers to simple and fundamental numbers), and planetary and numerical symbolism can also be used to interpret numbers and words; i.e. 76 can be interpreted as (7) – Venus (6) – Sun, thus 76 indicates a relationship between Sun and Venus.

Where a number has a 1 on either side of it, as in 111, 121, 131 etc., this number indicates a power acting in balanced manifestation (example: 141 = ELEMENTS, and also CONTINUOUS).

An additional technique is technically known as 'counting well', a reference to *Liber AL*: 'Count well its name and it shall be to you as 718'. In this technique, every letter of one word is added to every letter of another word. The speediest method of doing this is by the formula 'value of word A times number of letters in word B, and vice versa'. However, for various reasons which will emerge in the course of this book it is often performed longhand on a grid, with the letters of word A across the top, those of word B down the side, and the totals of their combinations entered in the appropriate sub-square.

Once one is possessed of these techniques (and it must be admitted that a computer programme is a very handy, though by no means indispensable, item), the purely theoretical side of the English Qaballa is your oyster. Even so, it must be emphasised that there is enough material available, after even a superficial examination of *Liber AL* through the Qaballa, to reveal outlines of a practical magical system beyond any known before.

This system interrelates certain dominant trends of Thelemic occultism. It does so on a very sophisticated level, which requires commitment, experience and resourcefulness of its exponents. Ideally, these exponents should work together, contributing their various skills, and some of them at least must possess Qaballistic and Astrological skills developed to a fine degree.

The following table should go some way toward emphasising the importance of astrological skills; whilst it should be noted that not all of the words appear in Class A texts, they are English words by adoption and are fundamental to the nature of the texts. The table is worth thorough examination and committing to memory.

Note that the sum of the planetary values is 813, which those with knowledge of the Hebrew Kabbalah will recognise as the value of the word ARARITA – the word of the Holy Hexagram which is used to invoke the planetary forces in the rites of the Golden Dawn and its derivatives.

ELEMENTAL VALUATIONS

Earth – 66	Fire – 78	Air – 36	Water – 65

ZODIACAL VALUATIONS

Aries – 66	Taurus – 76	Gemini – 117	Cancer – 78
Leo – 34	Virgo – 63	Libra – 58	Scorpio – 93
Sagittarius – 146	Capricorn – 121	Aquarius – 95	Pisces – 97

PLANETARY VALUATIONS

Sun – 36	Moon – 49	Mercury – 115	Venus – 71
Mars – 39	Jupiter – 143	Saturn – 73	Uranus – 66
Neptune – 145	Pluto – 76	Fortuna – 93	

If we subtract 36, the value of SUN, or Self at the centre, we have a number describing the system he experiences: 813 – 36 = 777. This idea of 'subtracting the Sun' is a key one; in astrology it appears in the formula for discovering the position of FORTUNA: Ascendant plus Moon minus Sun. In Crowley's terminology it compares with the 'slain lion' spoken of in the Amalantrah workings, in the writings of Blavatsky it is termed 'Solar Pralaya', and elsewhere we find it referred to as the 'Black Sun' – all convergent symbols.

777: Traditionally the number of the Flaming Sword or creative Lightning Flash of the Kabbalists which, when overlain on the Tree of Life, touches each Sephira in turn and certain paths, with a total value of 777.

777: The Goddess in Triple Form ISIS-BABALON-NUIT.

777: The ultimate extension of the perfect number (7), itself a symbol of wholeness and completion.

THE CIPHER OF AL

4 6 3 8 ABK 2 4 ALGMOR 3 Y
X (24) (89) RPSTOVAL.
What meaneth this, o prophet? Thou knowest
not; nor shalt thou know ever. There cometh
one to follow thee: he shall expound it. But
remember, o chosen one, to be me; to follow the
love of Nu in the star-lit heaven; to look forth
upon men, to tell them this glad word.

AL.II.76.

THE SOLUTION OF THE CIPHER OF II.76 HAS BEEN A PERENNIAL
problem of Thelemic Qabalism ever since AL was
dictated to Aleister Crowley by Aiwass in 1904. To put
this in perspective, let us quote from some of Crowley's
various commentaries on this enigmatic verse:

'A final revelation. The revealer to come is perhaps
the one mentioned in I.55. and III.47. The verse goes on
to urge the prophet to identify himself with Hadit, to
practice the union with Nu, and to proclaim this joyful
revelation unto men.'

'Verse 76 appears to be a Qabalistic test (on the
regular pattern) of any person who may claim to be the
magical heir of the Beast. Be ye well assured all, that
the solution, when it is found will be unquestionable. It
will be marked by the most sublime simplicity, and carry
immediate conviction'.

Of first importance are the qualifiers: 'perhaps' and 'appears to be'. Certainly *AL* mentions a 'child of thy bowels', 'his child & that strangely' and 'one to follow thee', and other cryptic references of like sort. In what sense this individual could be said to be Crowley's successor is rather a moot point. Indeed, are we justified in assuming these varied references all relate to only one individual?

There is then the question of 'a Qabalistic test (on the regular pattern)'. What is the regular pattern? Or rather what, if anything, did Crowley suppose it to be? There is no such pattern blazingly apparent in the G∴D∴ tradition, for example, which has to be considered Crowley's main influence in such matters. The only outstanding example of a cipher in the G∴D∴ tradition is the rather crude 'Cipher MS' from which their rites and Anna Sprengel's address were allegedly translated. This cipher is of such a transparently simplistic nature as to exclude serious comparison with II.76. The analogy drawn between II.76 and the rim of the Sigillum Aemeth elsewhere in this book might be apt, but the methods employed in relation to the Seal are not 'marked by the most sublime simplicity'. The 'Bacon cipher' style manipulations involved in extrapolating the Names of the Great Elemental Kings, or the Sigils of the Vast and Mighty Overseer Angels, from the Enochian Watchtowers and the Seal of Truth can hardly be said to 'carry immediate conviction' to most sane persons.

The only such 'regular patterns' which are truly comparable are to be found in Graves' *White Goddess*. In this work Graves portrays the complex and jumbled clues to the nature of various ritual alphabets of antiquity.

(That some of his work is pseudo-historical is not germane here.) The riddling alphabetical mysteries he describes do not resemble II.76 much either. However, the legendary characters who have solved such riddles have achieved religious status of one sort or another, and the nature of their solutions might very well be taken as indicative of II.76's significance.

Whatever Crowley may have meant by a 'Qabalistic test (on the regular pattern)', it seems to me the only useful attitude to take is that the test is not of a person, but of a potential 'English Qaballa'. If there can be found to be a close relationship between the structure of the qaballistic alphabet and II.76, then the test's primary conditions will have been met. Here the comparison with *The Song of Amergin* riddle, described by Graves, becomes more appropriate, since in that story whoever unjumbles the verses and explains the ambiguities discovers the order of the alphabet.

It seems obvious to me that no solution whatsoever will be self-evident to all. Imagine two Thelemites agreeing on any matter of even half the apparent significance of this verse! Add to this difficulty the fact that the person whose solution is deemed to be correct is 'entitled' to the 'dignity' of being recognised as Crowley's successor and the scope for contention is magnified not twice but a thousandfold. Crowley believed at least for a time that the 'child' was Frater Achad, who discovered not the English Qaballa, but a significant key word which produced some intriguing results when applied to some of *AL*'s puzzles.

This word was AL, from which *The Book of the Law* (formerly, and in many ways more appropriately, called 'L') takes its present technical name. It is my belief that this keyword is even more significant than Achad or Crowley realised, being in fact 'the key of it all' or rather 'the key of it: AL'. The problem was that the key was not placed in the lock, the lock being the ordinary order of the English Alphabet. However Achad came within a whisker of discovering English Qaballa himself as we can see from this interesting entry in his record of the time:

"'LAW' is LA (Nuit-Hadit) completed by W= [Hebrew Vau spelt in full], the Son RHK in His dual aspect as Horus-Harpocrates. Also Vau is the Hierophant 'Hoor in His secret name and splendour is the Lord Initiatory.'"

Had Achad been a little more proficient with ciphers he might have noted ALW forming the beginning of the 11-fold order of the English Alphabet. This is the more intriguing when we consider the importance of Aleph (ALP in Hebrew) in both Achad and Crowley's work on *The Book of the Law*. If we consider both LA-W and AL-P: LAW gives us the keywords AL and LA, and also the Order and Value hinted at in 'Azure Lidded Woman', while ALP gives the keyword AL and LA but also the last letter of the English Qaballistic series. Writing the Order and Value in a circle we would find the letters of LAW and of ALP placed together.

We turn now to the discovery of EQ and its relationship to certain frameworks found in the manuscript of *AL* itself. The 'order & value' was discovered by an esoteric Order in the United Kingdom who had magically sought it out. They ritualised their

intention to discover it and set to work to do so. First they
came up with ABC = 1 2 3 etc. and various other dead
ends. These they ritually burnt; soon after one of them
noted that counting eleven letters from A we obtain L,
thus AL. This process was continued until the order
A L W H S D O Z K V G R C N Y J U F Q B M X I T E P
was 'obtained'. So far, so good; next they turned to the
mysterious grid on sheet 16 of *AL* III. in the manuscript
of *AL*. There are two ways of writing the alphabet on
this grid, down or across. If we go across we get:

A	B	C	D	E	F	G	H
I	J	K	L	M	O	P	Q
Q	R	S	T	U	V	W	X
Y	Z	A	B	C	D	E	F
G	H	I	J	K	L	M	N
O	P	Q	R	S	T	U	V
W	X	Y	Z	A	B	C	D
E	F	G	H	I	J	K	L
M	N	O	P	Q	R	S	T
U	V	W	X	Y	Z	A	B

The diagonals give an order well known to
numerologists:

1	2	3	4	5	6	7	8	9
A	B	C	D	E	F	G	H	I
J	K	L	M	N	O	P	Q	R
S	T	U	V	W	X	Y	Z	

This order and value does not produce any particularly useful or interesting results when applied to *AL*, but it is intriguing that the grid should produce such a recognisable pattern. Now look at what happens when we write the alphabet down the grid:

A	K	U	E	O	Y	I	S
B	L	V	F	P	Z	J	T
C	M	W	G	Q	A	K	U
D	N	X	H	R	B	L	V
E	O	Y	I	S	C	M	W
F	P	Z	J	T	D	N	X
G	Q	A	K	U	E	O	Y
H	R	B	L	V	F	P	Z
I	S	C	M	W	G	Q	A
J	T	D	N	X	H	R	B

The diagonals give A L W H S D O Z K V G R C N Y J U F Q B M X I T E P. Note that diagonals ascending from the left side of the grid give the AJS order, and that the other grid gives ALW in alternate diagonal squares upwards. More curious still, there are 2 geometrical stars of 26 points which convert ABC into ALW and vice versa, and two stars that produce AJS and vice versa, and a fifth that creates and uncreates a third order, AFK. The AJS is a ninefold progression, the ALW an elevenfold and the AFK a fivefold progression. The AFK order requires 'knight's moves' to be formed on the grid as it exists in *AL*. Unfortunately, I do not know for certain where or why the AJS order originates in 'traditional' numerology, although Regardie and/or the G∴.D∴. have been credited with it.

These permutations of the English alphabet seem to be significant in some respect. It has been noted that a grid one line shorter will produce several permutations of the alphabet, including those mentioned above. Certainly odd numbered permutations of the English Alphabet share some significant qualities. An example of this shared significance is the fact that all such 'cipher alphabets' give the same numerical value to the name ISIS.

There has been a certain amount of work done by various parties with these alternative orders, but none has produced results as significant as the ALW order. This is to some extent the fault of the experimenters, who have flawed their findings by using their pseudo-ciphers on words which are a) outside *AL* and the *Holy Books*, and b) outside the English Language! Such words as Yesod and Aleph hardly require an English Qaballa for amplification. Despite these early failures I suspect that the permutations will eventually produce some significant results, and that it is worthwhile examining them.

The full range of permutations (1, 3, 5, 7, 9, 11 – 15, 17, 19, 21, 23, 25, and 27-fold) can be written as a Table of Permutations in a similar fashion to that depicted in Agrippa and his plagiarist Barrett, to produce Barbarous Names and to disguise 'Statements of Intent' or 'Sentences of Desire' from the conscious mind. Rendered pronounceable with judicious use of the Wakanaba method (see page 111) we obtain an extremely satisfactory modern application of an archaic technique.

So much for the nature and structure of the cipher, the alphabet and the matter of the grid of sheet sixteen of Chapter III. in the manuscript of *AL*. It falls to me now to describe the relations between II.76 and English Qaballa. Applying EQ to the cipher of II.76 we obtain the total value of 351. This number has some interesting entries in Crowley's Hebrew *Sepher Sephiroth* which we will leave to the reader to seek out. What is more significant for our purposes (for I dislike comparisons between gematrias in distinct languages, even in cases as fundamental as this) is the fact that 351 is the sum of the numbers 1 to 26, the number of letters in the English Alphabet, and consequently of the values attributed to the letters. Thus is established a close connection between II.76 and EQ by simple addition. If we consult the manuscript of *AL* and examine II.76 we find that the cipher is in two lines, thus:

4 6 3 8 ABK 2 4 ALGMOR 3 Y
X (24) (89) RPSTOVAL.

The first line consists of seventeen numbers and letters, the second of eleven. If we multiply 17 by 11, as suggested perhaps by the x at the beginning of line two, we obtain 187. This is the value of the phrase ENGLISH ALPHABET (from *AL* II.55), and also of the words FOUR ONE EIGHT. This is indeed significant, since by the first method, addition, we obtained the value of the series 1 to 26, and here, by a curious 'coincidence', we obtain by multiplication the name of the series. The cipher demonstrates mathematically the veracity of English Qaballa. However, there are other curious properties of this string of numbers and 'words', as will be demonstrated below. The more abstruse development of this material is not 'marked by the most sublime simplicity', it may not 'carry immediate conviction', but it has shown itself to be of remarkable value, and may yet prove to be the most important aspect of EQ.

Let's begin with some simple gematria. Crowley's commentary to II.76 includes the preceding verse II.75: 'Aye, listen to the numbers & the words.' LISTEN = 93, whilst NUMBERS & THE WORDS = 200. The verse in its entirety adds to 418. This, as we will see elsewhere, is the number of LIBRA + SCORPIO + SAGITTARIUS + CAPRICORN. It is also, in Thelemic Tradition, the number of the Great Work, as well as the value of ABRAHADABRA when spelt with Hebrew letters by Crowley, and of ABRA % HADABRA in EQ, and as seen above, the words FOUR ONE EIGHT are equivalent by gematria to the phrase ENGLISH ALPHABET. For now let us simply bear in mind the numbers 93 and 200 in relation to the astrological factors Libra and Scorpio.

$4 + 6 + 3 + 8 + A + B + K + 2 + 4 + A = 58 =$
LIBRA, HADIT, etc.

$L + G + M + O + R + 3 + Y + X = 93 =$
SCORPIO, DIVIDE, TIME, TAHUTI, etc.

$(24) + (89) + R + P + S + T + O + V + A + L = 200 =$
MANIFESTATION.

What we have here are two sets of ten, one balanced (LIBRA) and unmanifest (HADIT), the other manifested (MANIFESTATION) in the realm of duality (200). These two are divided (DIVIDE) by 93. The Name TAHUTI in this context is more than a little reminiscent of the G∴D∴ documents (echoed in *Liber Pyramidos* and *Liber Israfel*) entitled 'The General and Particular Exordium'. Before turning to these, it is worth remembering where Tahuti's name occurs in the Class A, AL.II.39: 'A feast for Tahuti and the child of the Prophet – secret, O Prophet.' This, of course, is a reference to the 'one to follow thee.' Now let us turn to the Golden Dawn documents aforementioned, which I shall quote in their entirety. The passages of special relevance are in bold type.

THE GENERAL EXORDIUM

'The Speech in the Silence:
The Words against the Son of Night;
The Voice of Thoth before the Universe in the presence of the eternal Gods;
The Formulas of Knowledge;
The Wisdom of Breath;
The Radix of Vibration;
The Shaking of the Invisible;
The Rolling Asunder of the Darkness;
The Becoming Visible of Matter;
The Piercing of the Coils of the Stooping Dragon;
The Breaking forth of the Light;
All these are in the Knowledge of Tho-oth.'

The Particular Exordium

'At the Ending of the Night,
At the Limits of the Light,
Tho-oth stood before the Unborn Ones of Time!
Then was formulated the Universe;
Then came forth the Gods thereof,
The Aeons of the Bornless Beyond;
Then was the Voice vibrated;
Then was the Name declared.

At the Threshold of the Entrance,
Between the Universe and the Infinite,
In the Sign of the Enterer, stood Tho-oth,
As before him were the Aeons proclaimed.
In Breath did he vibrate them;
In Symbols did he record them;
For betwixt the Light and the Darkness did he stand.'

It is perhaps unnecessary to remark that Thoth/
Tho-oth is identical with Tahuti. These documents
form the basis of the G∴D∴'s cosmogony and 'creation
myth', so that it is quite startling to find II.76, an
apparently meaningless string of letters and numbers,
echoing them quite so forcibly.

The Universe is of course represented by 200 =
MANIFESTATION, whilst the Infinite is designated
Fifty-Eight. II.76 accordingly represents Two 'Trees'
separated by 93. The first Tree is the Unmanifest World,
perfect, balanced and 'Bornless'. The second Tree is the
'Tree of Life' as we generally understand the term. This
is quite in accord with old Kabbalistic tradition, since
before Malkuth came into being Da'ath was a Sephirah
in its own right. It is the falling of Da'ath that creates

Malkuth. The Lodge of the A∴A∴ responsible for the discovery of EQ went a great deal further than this in their exegesis of II.76. In order to understand what is to follow, the student will need to be wide awake, and possessed of considerable qaballistic savvy. Rather than try and explain the hermeneutic processes used, I will simply give the material as it stands. As said above, this material is by no means self-explanatory. I shall simply have to presume that enough material of interest has been laid before the reader to show that the effort of coming to grips with what is to follow is effort well spent.

If we have to LISTEN (=93) to the numbers and the words, how are we going to go about it? Mumbling this string of letters and numbers as a mantra is not particularly productive, so what else can we do? The rationale of the Qaballists who first discovered EQ, and set to work on the by no means enviable task of clarifying II.76, seems to have been: since some mathematical process is certainly implied by this 'Qabalistic test (on the regular pattern)', we can add 93 = LISTEN to the various numbers and letters.

Whilst the results are not immediately self-explanatory, they do have a certain internal consistency. By this I mean that the values thus obtained recur in our study of the Class A texts with EQ in places of critical importance, so that we are more ready to admit the importance of their discoveries, even if – separated in time and understanding as we are – we do not altogether understand how these calculations and decisions came to be made in the first place. As the historian of the birth of a Qaballistic system, my task is, like theirs, unenviable. It is also, one concedes, a unique and indeed a privileged position. But I digress. So: applying EQ to II.76 we get:

$$4\ 6\ 3\ 8\ ABK\ 2\ 4\ A = 58 = LIBRA$$
$$LGMOR\ 3\ YX = 93 = SCORPIO$$
$$(24)(89)RPSTOVAL = 200 = MANIFESTATION$$

The number 93 represents the menstrual flux in woman, SCORPIO; the whole formula being LIBRA SCORPIO SAGITTARIUS CAPRICORN = 418. A table explaining how this formula works out on various levels concludes this chapter (first published in *The New Equinox*, Vol.6 No.1). 93 is of course the value of the word Thelema in Greek, and this is the Word of the Law. If II.76 represents a universal formula, which is to say 'the creation of the world', then the word LISTEN applied to the NUMBERS & THE WORDS (= 200 i.e. MANIFESTATION) seems to mean that we are subject to the Law of Thelema.

Adding 93 to each number in the 'Manifestation' part of II.76 we get:

(1)	(2)	(3)	(4)	(5)	(6)	(7)	(8)	(9)	(10)
24	89	R	P	S	T	O	V	A	L
117	182	105	119	98	117	100	103	94	95

Cult Mnemonic from Gematrias on the Manifest Tree: 'The Mystery of Restriction is the Blessing of Creation; Mighty Fortune is Queen, Her Eternal Sister is Her Beloved.'

These numbers are then taken as the key numbers of the Sephiroth (see numbers in brackets for Sephirothic correspondences). Applying the same rule to the Libra section of the Cipher we obtain:

(1)	(2)	(3)	(4)	(5)	(6)	(7)	(8)	(9)	(10)
4	6	3	8	A	B	K	2	4	A
97	99	96	101	94	113	102	95	97	94

Cult Mnemonic from Gematrias on the Perfect Tree: 'Nothing – Divided but Virginal – The Mystic Sphinx of the Spirit; Beauty and Delight are Nothing and Her Sister.'

The number 58 = HADIT = LIBRA. In *AL*, Hadit says: 'I am perfect, being (= 93) Not;' Libra is the sign of The Balance. The LIBRA/HADIT Tree is perfect, so the tenth sphere is in the 'Da'ath' position to give the perfect and original form of the Tree.

The number 200 = MANIFESTATION or duality (2). Nuit, who is None and Two, says in *AL* I.29: 'I am divided for love's sake'. In the next verse, we find the 'PAIN OF DIVISION' = 200 = MANIFESTATION. The means by which Zero manifests is the Tree of Life, therefore we have the 'trees of Eternity' (*AL* I.59) divided by 93. As will be seen by the qaballistically inclined Thelemic magician, this schema follows *AL* in its interpretation of manifestation. Consider the 'Creation Myth' of AL in I.28 (28 = WORD):

NONE BREATHED THE LIGHT FAINT AND FAERY OF THE STARS...
60 117 117 80 71

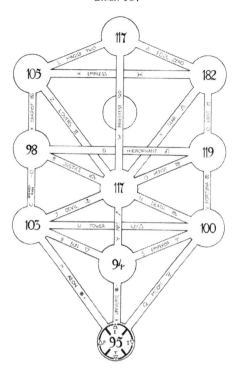

THE TREE OF MANIFESTATION
(FOR MORE ON THE TWO TREES, SEE PAGE 107)

On the Tree of Manifestation, Kether and Tiphereth have the same numeration (God the Father = God the Son, to use the language of the Old Aeon), which is 117 = HOOR PAAR KRAAT. Consider this proposition: if NONE, i.e. Zero, is the Qaballistic Ain Soph, the next word must indicate the number 1 or Kether, and 117 is the value arrived at for Kether by the process outlined above. None is Nothing, and NOTHING = 97 = RA HOOR KHUT, the top and bottom of the Unmanifest Tree (p. 110), which begins and ends in NOTHING, logically enough.

Strictly, however, NONE = 60 = DEATH, which relates to Scorpio (93), equated with the House of Death in Astrology. This is too complex a subject to enter into here, where we are already in way over most folk's heads, including mine! The NONE = DEATH aspect of this formula applies to the Grade of Magister Templi, whereas this chapter is written primarily for Adeptus Minors or those aspiring to that Grade.

It will be seen that various spheres involved in this exposition have the same numerical value, and there may just be a correlation here with some of Grant's ideas concerning a Two Tree system, though this is not an analogy I wish to push too far. Whether or not these numerations indicate a particular affinity between these spheres is a fascinating area for speculation and experiment, but it should be borne in mind that the Two Trees are Divided by 93, and the interrelations between them depend to some degree on particular stellar configurations. When these aspects or positions occur, the 93 Current is activated and energy flows out of Manifestation to the Perfect Tree and vice versa. If this did not occur then Destiny would be fixed, and astrology would work uninterrupted on a race of automatons, such as Adam and Eve appear to have been before the intervention of the Serpent of Genesis.

Indeed, things could be even worse than this, but they are not. Destiny so-called can be aborted, magical effects can be created, and Change can and does occur. In the case of a single Tree, such as is vulgarly imagined by uninitiated Qabalists, Life itself would be virtually impossible. Nothing could occur in the realm of manifestation beyond the creation of unicellular organisms – this is logical if you think about it, since a Tree going from Zero to manifestation could only produce this at best without periodic interference from outside the system. This is why the deities of Initiation possess dual characteristics, such as Baphomet, the twin-sexed DOUBLE-POWERED deity of the Magicians.

Having said that the work of Kenneth Grant bears some vague resemblance to elements of EQ, it is worth tracing briefly where these distinct paths overlap, and where they diverge. Grant's focus on the role of the Priestess in magical work finds parallels in our own, as it does in the works of Culling and Bardon. The Two Trees are the closest point of contact between Grant's system and the EQ, but there are ample traces of such a schema in the older Qaballistic texts, in AL itself and elsewhere. The extreme point of divergence between Grant's work and that of the English Qaballists is in actual practice. Grant's work is unmistakably on the extreme borders of occultism, with no safeguards to prevent delusion. English Qaballa and its magical methods have the yardstick of pure number to avoid the pitfalls (colloquially known as Choronzon) of the 93 Current.

There is a limit to how much accurate information can be obtained from Astral work alone, due to the nature of the thing itself. Only pure number can reveal the truth, and it is part of the Thelemic tradition that astral visions should ALWAYS be checked by pure number to ensure validity. It is against the background of pure number that the Class A material must be examined to avoid similar pitfalls. At the end of the second chapter of AL it is said: 'They shall worship thy name, foursquare, mystic, wonderful, the number of the man; and the name of thy house 418.' THY HOUSE = 101, MYSTIC = 101. This suggests that the House in question is the House of the dual one, for 1 + 0 + 1 = 2, while 101 is the value of various double symbols such as ELEVEN, PILLAR + WORLD, DOUBLE WAND, and WANDED ONE (from the expression Double Wanded One); also SOLVE COAGULA, the double formula which is found engraved on images of Baphomet.

The dual one is of course this same BAPHOMET (= 128 = THE BEAST, SCARLET WOMAN, SUN AND VENUS and ORDEAL X) expressed in the Zodiac as CAPRICORN = 121 = balanced duality. The importance of Capricorn is as the final stage in the Libra-Scorpio-Sagittarius-Capricorn cycle. During the Sun's transit through these signs, the candidate in the Ordeal X experiences and resolves the conflicts or dualities in their nature, to emerge in Capricorn as a child – or even a manifestation – of Baphomet. This is the meaning of the title applied to Baphomet in old literature, the frequently misunderstood REX MUNDI or Lord of the Earth. The triumphant and revitalised initiate, the CROWNED CHILD = 128.

SUBJECT	LIBRA	SCORPIO	SAGITTARUIS	CAPRICORN
Sun-Venus Magician	Candidate	Ordeal X	Integration	Thelemite
Woman	Unfertilized Seed	Menstrual Flux	Rest	Renewed Woman
Christ	Judgment	Crucifixion (N.B. Mysteries of the Crucifixion = 418)	Mysterious Three Days	Resurrection
Christian	Sin vs. Self	Repentance	Redemption	Christian
Nature	Harvest	Apparent Death of Nature	Rest	Green Man (Potential for renewal)
Mind	World/Ego Conflict	Neurosis	Breakdown, Upsurge of Unconscious Forces	Catharsis
Existence	Life	Death	Rest	Rebirth
Evolution	Evolutionary Stasis	Conversion of Species	Consolidation of Adaptation	New Variety
Science	Problem	Intense Study	Rest	Solution
Nations	Conflict	War (Negotiations)	Armistice (Agreement)	Peace
Health	Disease	Treatment	Rest	Renewal
Day	Activity	Onset of Sleep	Rest	Renewal
Mystic	Illumination	Dark Night of the Soul	Realisation	Prophet
Thelemite	Names Enemy in Libra-Scorpio	Enemy cast into "93"	Silence	Free of Enemy
Minor Adept	Names all the things he does not want - enemies	Enemies are destroyed, leaving vacuum in experience and consciousness	Vacuum is filled by "what the enemies are not", i.e., that considered advantageous to the Magician's Will	Will of the Magician fulfilled

PART TWO

The system of Qabalah used in this book is neither 19th century nor medieval Hebrew, a fact that has caused many traditionalists to reject it out of hand. The loss is theirs, since this system makes accessible features of the older systems which 19th Century occultism was unable to deliver to us. This is because this system, rather than trying to fit together a collection of relics, begins afresh, and having done so achieves that which has daunted the curators of the 'museum of magic' for too long.

– from *Liber 187*

QABALLISTIC MAGICK

'Hidden in the labyrinth of the Alphabet is my
Sacred Name, the Sigil of all things unknown.'
The Anathema of ZOS, Austin Spare

KABBALISTIC MAGICK – BY WHICH WE MEAN NOT THE GOLDEN
Dawn variant (Qabalah) but the magick associated
with the Hebrew Kabbalah and its ancestors – was
chiefly concerned with obtaining access to various
planes of being. The 'standard' Tree of Life is neither
the sole nor even the chief example of a 'map' of such
planes in the historical development of the system.
The Gnostic ascent through the heavens has much in
common with the original form of Kabbalistic magick
and the more contemporary 'rising on the planes'
practised by Crowley, Florence Farr et al. In particular,
Crowley's exploration of the Thirty Aethyrs of the
Enochian system approximates more to this kind of
magick than do the various forms of 'path-working'
extant in modern occult circles.

The visionary experiences undergone in these
adventures of the spirit were attended by the most
frightful psychic or (as we might say today with little if
any amplification of meaning) psychological pressures.
The unworthy or unsuitable experimenter with these
methods was literally assaulted by armed angelic
agencies. Some of the descriptions in *The Vision and the
Voice* are remarkably similar to some of the old literature

of the Hebrew Kabbalah. When Crowley describes
the efforts of the Angels to exclude him by force from
experiences to which his degree of initiation did not
entitle him, he could be quoting directly from the books
of the Merkabah tradition which preceded the medieval
Kabbalah. The use of 'Words of Power' and other keys
to reduce or deflect these assaults is a common feature
of these works. Similarly, in the Gnostic world view, the
initiate had to ascend through the planetary heavens
before reaching more exalted levels of being. The
final stage was suffering the experience of face to face
intercourse with the King of Heaven.

All this may seem a long way off from *The Book
of the Law*, but is this really so? The Qaballa of *AL* is
intimately concerned not only with practical magick in
the accepted sense of 'results magick' but with the most
exalted states of consciousness to which the initiate can
aspire. Certainly the conception of deity contained in
Liber AL is distinct from that of the Judaeo-Christian
complex. Nevertheless, a qaballistic approach to *The
Book of the Law* will inevitably lead to such visionary
experiences, and dealings with various agencies on the
thresholds of the sanctuaries of 'inner knowledge'.

These sanctuaries are guarded, as we have said, by
the most potent forms of spiritual agency conceivable.
Only a thorough mastery of the Qaballa will enable the
initiate to pass within, and this may take many years to
acquire. However, the proper performance of astrological
magick, in the best sense – be it the therapeutic astro-
magic of Marsilio Ficino the Renaissance Neoplatonist,
or the initiatory magick of the Sun-Venus – will be
of enormous value in acquiring the psychic integrity

required to satisfy the guardians of these sanctuaries, and indeed to pass through the initial levels. In other words, astrological initiation is the interior equivalent of the passwords involved in the Gnostic ascent through the planetary heavens before approaching the deeper levels of the psyche (or of the cosmological model).

This might seem a little out of the way for many modern occultists, and perhaps offensive to the atheistic or rationalistic perspectives held by many of them. All I will say in mitigation is that the worldview of ancient Gnosticism and medieval Kabbalah is the best approximation to the techniques and experiences involved with this system that I am able to find. Furthermore, since an enormous literature exists on the subject, with an advanced critical apparatus, I am not loath to make use of it. The fact that magick does not adapt itself easily to modern scientific language, or to rationalistic psychological viewpoints, is not my main concern. My efforts are directed towards making available a sophisticated modern magical methodology. The fact is that this 'system', if I may use such an ugly word, is similar in nature to some of the most evolved systems of the past, which have been neglected or misunderstood by contemporary occultists, and still more by contemporary psychologists and their ilk. Those who have made a deep study of the older systems may be able to appreciate the enormity of my undertaking.

English Qaballa is, in essence, a modern astro-qaballistic system. It has points of contact with older systems such as Tantra, Kabbalah and Gnosticism, all of which are themselves related, both historically and in their motivation and method. It resumes the modus

operandi and other elements of its ancient forebears,
yet differs from them in one essential respect.

Whereas the systems of the past are divided from us
by a gulf of language, cultural perspective and religious
outlook, the EQ is connected to us through the most
significant text in modern magical history, uses our own
language, and seeks to communicate with us in terms
suited to our times. This notwithstanding, the use of
prayer in modern magick is not without its traducers.
Since it has become increasingly fashionable to see the
old gods as impersonal archetypal forces devoid of any
life of their own outside our own consciousness, we must
define our terms very carefully to avoid entering into
futile debates over the nature of the forces behind AL.
The finest definition available is that in *Liber O*:

'In this book it is spoken of Sephiroth, and the
Paths, of Spirits and Conjurations; of Gods, Spheres,
Planes, and many other things which may or may not
exist. It is immaterial whether they exist or not. By
doing certain things certain results follow; students
are most earnestly warned against attributing objective
reality or philosophical validity to any of them.'

The prime example of such results is *The Book of
the Law* itself, the direct result of a series of invocations
performed in Cairo in 1904. That the *Book* contains
sufficient data at a cursory glance (provided the
frame of reference exists to understand it on its own
terms) to prove itself beyond the means of normal
consciousness to produce is indisputable. What is not
beyond dispute, though the purpose of such dispute
is questionable, is the means of transmission, granted
that they were extraordinary.

THE MAGICAL ALPHABET

'There will be born at London English folk whose mantra for worship is in the Phiranga (English) language, who will be undefeated in battle and Lords of the World.' Merutantra, XXIII *Prakasha* (17th century).

THE SO-CALLED COLLECTIVE CONSCIOUSNESS OF MANKIND is in fact a genetically inherent mathematical and linguistic model capable of encoding and transmitting a qaballistic text through an individual consciousness under extreme conditions, and after much training. The Jungian collective unconscious, or as Eliphas Levi termed it 'the Astral Light' or 'Luminiferous Ether', is a means by which transpersonal impressions can be transmitted or experienced, which has been held to explain certain psychological and occult phenomenon. What neither Jung nor Levi realised was that their theory has a biological basis which permits a scientific conception of Qaballistic ideas. It is significant that Levi's concept is still employed even in such modern magical formulations as Carroll's *Chaos Magick Theory*. An interesting light on Qaballistic ideas may be found in *Chance and Necessity* by Jacques Monod, as well as in the ideas of Chomsky; we quote here from Monod, *Evolution*, Ch.7, p.128:

'Anatomical evidence confirms the idea that the primary acquisition of language is bound up with a process of epigenetic development. It is known that the maturing of the brain continues after birth but halts at puberty. This development seems to consist mainly in a considerable amplification of the network of interconnections between cortical neurons... it is a small step, which I personally am prepared to take, to the theory that if, in the child, the acquisition of language appears so miraculously spontaneous it is because it is an integral part of an epigenetic development one of whose functions is to prepare for language. To be a little more precise: the development of the cognitive function itself depends, beyond any doubt, upon this postnatal growth of the cortex. It is the acquisition of language in the course of this epigenesis that makes for its association with the cognitive function – an association so intimate that it is very difficult to separate, by introspection, the utterance from the thought it expounds... the capacity for language can no longer be regarded as a superstructure. It must be conceded that, between the cognitive functions and the symbolic language they beget – and through which they are articulated – there is in modern man a close symbiosis which can only be the product of lengthy common evolution...' According to Chomsky and his school, linguistic analysis in depth reveals one basic 'form' common to all human languages, beneath their boundless diversity.

Chomsky says this form must be considered innate and characteristic of the species. Certain philosophers or anthropologists have been shocked by this thesis, and see it as a return to Cartesian metaphysics.

Provided its implicit biological content be accepted, I see nothing whatsoever wrong with it. On the contrary, it strikes me as a most natural conclusion, once one assumes that the evolution of man's cortical structures could not but be influenced by a capacity for language acquired very early and in the crudest possible state. This amounts to assuming that spoken language, when it appeared among primitive mankind, not only made possible the evolution of culture but contributed decisively to man's physical evolution.

This shows that Qaballistic magick belongs fairly and squarely in the 21st century – with a firm philosophical basis behind it – though considerable dead-weight requires pruning. In particular it is absurd that traditionalists should cling to what Umberto Eco calls 'the crusty old myth of Hebrew as the original language'. This primacy cannot seriously be maintained in any sense but that of unhistorical metaphor, and is adduced by these same 'traditionalists' solely as an excuse for their failure to transcend an outmoded cultural model. Even the claim of Northern Semitic to be the earliest hieratic alphabet (a different matter entirely from a hieratic language) is somewhat suspect in the light of substantial evidence that Northern Semitic was not an alphabet but a syllabary, making Greek the first true alphabet as such:

'It has long been customary to attribute this revolutionary culmination to the Semites, four main divisions of whose so-called alphabet – the Ethiopic... and the Aramaic, the Canaanite, and the Palestinian – were in use about 1000 BC, each consisting of from 22 to 30 signs, all of them expressing consonants. This Semitic practice... of omitting vowels was almost certainly copied from the ancient Egyptians...' as I.J. Gelb maintains in his penetrating analysis, A *Study of Writing* (London, 1952), and in support of which contention he produces convincing arguments and evidence, it is difficult to escape the conclusion that the early Egyptian and Semitic writings were in fact syllabic, and that their phonetic signs represented not merely consonants, but consonants plus any vowel... It would thus appear that it was the Greeks who evolved the first true alphabet, the Semitic origins of which, however [are] openly acknowledged by the Greeks themselves, who described their writing as Phoenician'. (*Lost Languages*, P. E. Cleator.)

It is certain that Sanskrit – very much a hieratic language – is far more ancient than Hebrew and Aramaic, and has been a great influence upon many languages including the vocabulary of Biblical Hebrew, and to a far larger extent upon English itself. Moreover the *Atharva Veda* employs numerical values for Sanskrit and is considerably older (1500 to 2000 BC) than both the Pentateuch (9th to 6th Century BC) and the first Greek gematric text, the works of Homer (11th to 7th Century BC).

Regarding the 'myth of original language', magicians of a more radical turn of mind, such as Frater U.D. (see his *Practical Sigil Magic*, Ch. 6, p. 64), when considering Austin Osman Spare's 'Alphabet of Desire' express the same anxiety about tradition though for opposite reasons. Frater U.D.'s concern appears to be that Spare's perception of the Magical Alphabet as part of a 'Proto-language' might be seen, in the phrase of Chomsky's critics, as a 'return to Cartesian metaphysics'.

This concern is not necessary, firstly since Spare considered it essential for the individual magician to devise the sigils of his/her own 'Alphabet'. More importantly, he also considered the 'proto-language' underlying this Alphabet to be biological in origin – indeed he went so far as to connect each letter of his 'Alphabet of Desire' with a sexual principle. This shows that the emphasis which Monod (a convinced materialist) placed upon the biological content of Chomsky's thesis was already acknowledged by Spare in his own work.

The importance of letter forms, whether in the 'Kabbalistic yoga' of Abraham Abulafia or the sigil magick of Austin Spare, is their effect on consciousness. This effect can be observed in various ways but in the end these are all one. Letter forms are potent concentration devices, and when emptied of content or conscious meaning are an excellent focus for meditation and trance induction. Their capacity to carry meaning ensures their fascination, thus making them effective foci for the conscious mind while their unintelligibility (when arranged in unintelligible sequences or combined in sigils, bind-runes, etc.) makes it far more difficult for the conscious mind to formulate distractions. Through the effective use of such forms we may enter the realm of the underlying 'proto-language' whereby mystical and magical effects are produced.

Obviously a 'bio-linguistic' model has further implications for practical occultism despite its philosophical subtleties. However, in the end this does not affect the magical practicalities; essentially, an intelligence exterior to any particular human consciousness was responsible for both *The Book of the Law* and its Qaballa. The 'Secret Chiefs' live not in some ethereal other-world but within the transpersonal realm of consciousness reflected in the Babel of human language. Later chapters of the current work resume some practical implications of this idea in modern magick, and the theme underlies the entire work.

QABALAH AS RITUAL LANGUAGE

'The creation of a ritual and Qabalistic method
for English is one of the major problems of the
Aeon of Horus.'
Bill Heidrick. O.T.O. Newsletter. Spring 1978

THE LEAST UNDERSTOOD ASPECT OF QABALAH IS ITS USE FOR
generating ritual structures; there is scarcely an element
of ceremonial magick that is not based on a Qabalistic
concept. This all-pervading influence goes far beyond
the specific Names invoked in a given ritual, extending
to matters as sublime or mundane as the hierarchies
worked with, the sigils traced, the colours employed, the
number of candles, the ingredients in the incense, the
time chosen for working, the conception of relations
between self, deity and cosmos, the position one stands
in and the direction one faces. That a system often
dismissed as 'games with numbers' is the ultimate source
of virtually every part of ritual magick, and much else
besides, is too often overlooked.

Qabalah has been ill served by both traditionalists
and radicals, many of the former endlessly repeating
fallacies of the 19th century and overlooking any
research done since, the latter mistaking the lethargy
of Qabalah's exponents for the obsolescence of
Qabalah itself. Few have appreciated either that
systems similar to the Qabalah have been a major
factor in the magical and mystical systems of a great
many other cultures; a striking example is to be found

in Tantra which is based as much on mantra and rising through levels of the cosmos as it is on sexual technique. In like fashion the essential form of the shamanic tradition consists of the ascent of a visionary ladder (often through possession of appropriate words) and has strong links to the Hebrew 'Work of the Chariot'.

The most simple and obvious way of using our own (the English) alphabet and language ideographically, i.e. magically rather than as a linear and pseudo-rational process, is in talismans and ritual magick. The sigils of Zos Kia Cultus are an obvious example. Similarly the runic alphabet, the direct ancestor of our English characters, is also ideal for this purpose. Likewise the symbols of *Liber Trigrammaton* may be used in talismanic and other 'traditional' ways, either as they are or as the basis of linear figures in much the same way as Francis Barrett and the Golden Dawn used the symbols of geomancy to obtain 'characters of the planets'. The process of 'counting well' described previously in this book provides a method of constructing Magick Squares and Rectangles; the idea being that the 'Practical Qaballist' will either discover the ones he needs or devise them, as and when a particular operation becomes necessary.

An example of how Qaballistic ideas and the idea of a 'cut-up', as developed by Brion Gysin and William Burroughs, can be combined into a potent magical tool is given here in a 'spell' based on the English Qaballistic gematria value of SUN + JUPITER = 179, the intention being to make a spell to invoke or celebrate that power while these heavenly bodies are in aspect. Words or phrases with the appropriate value, derived from *The Book of the Law* and/or from *The Holy*

Books of Thelema are then juxtaposed by a random/
non-random mental process producing a cut-up from
the original text (ideally a Book of Numbers should be
kept wherein the magician records important values
under numerical headings) which is magically linked
with the desired force.

There is a veil–raise the spell–of the double wand–

For I am Nothing–Glorious as the Sun–

Raise the spell–ye twin warriors—pillars of the world–of the

double wand–of the double wand–

A feast for life–never ending–glorious as the sun–is ever the
son–

Raise the spell–a feast for life–thy heart beat–never ending–

Raise the spell–and no other shall say nay–

Raise the spell–the key of it all–star & star-system–the white
foam–

That companion–never ending–SUN & JUPITER–RAISE
THE SPELL!

Zealous students will doubtless be able to apply
this technique for themselves; it should nevertheless
be noted that while cut-ups and English Qaballa are
contemporary magical tools, this modus operandi is
extremely traditional. This formula can obviously be
used for talismanic inscriptions. Here illustrated are two
examples of talismans as described above and elsewhere
in this book, one of JUPITER (values of 143), another of

SUN-JUPITER (values of 179). An appropriate verbal spell for use with these squares and talismans could be devised as above; alternatively or in addition this spell devised by AOS is extremely appropriate:

> O, mighty Rehctaw!
> Thou who exists in all erogenousness,
> We evoke Thee!
>
> By the power of the meanings
> Arising from these forms I make,
> We evoke Thee!
>
> By the Talismans that speak
> The secret leitmotif of desire,
> We evoke Thee!
>
> By the sacrifices, abstinences and transvaluations we make,
> We evoke Thee!
>
> By the sacred inbetweenness concepts
> Give us the flesh!
>
> We, who shall suffer all ecstasies,
> Give us the Will!
>
> By the quadriga sexualis
> Give us unvarying desire!
>
> By the conquest of fatigue
> Give us eternal resurgence!
>
> By the most sacred Word-graph of Heaven
> We invoke Thee!
>
> Amen.

Does all this take us any further into the actual use of *The Book of the Law* as it appears to require? Here the answer may at first seem to be not very much further. With or without having established the precise nature of the intelligence responsible for the writing of *The Book of the Law*, we are seemingly left with very few means of progress. One purpose of this book to make clear what these means of progress are.

Our purpose is not literary criticism but philosophical enquiry and a great deal more than that besides, and the careful reader will observe that the only obvious course is to follow much the same procedure as Crowley himself. Let us, then, establish two things. Firstly, what did Crowley do to attain the position of scribe? The answer here is simple enough. He undertook several years training: as a magician of the Golden Dawn; as a mystic in the Arab, Hindu and Buddhist traditions; and as a conventional western scholar of high academic standards (Bertrand Russell acknowledged him to have the best grasp of higher mathematics of any contemporary layman).

Consequently, he was ideally suited to undertake such an adventure, having the mental apparatus to try and understand the process of transmission and retain some degree of detachment. This is to understate the case, for what was happening in the writer's chair depended on his mystical and psychological training for success. Crowley had at his disposal a deep knowledge and experience of transcendental psychology via his Buddhist studies, and a wide range of magical and mystical techniques culled from a dozen cultural perspectives and reduced to a science by his able hand. In this way Crowley understood what was happening, and by similar means so may we all.

When we speak of magical techniques, we are not necessarily concerned with objective results. What we are speaking of, in the context of this discussion so far, is the scientific fact that certain techniques produce alterations in consciousness, and with luck and training, access particular areas of consciousness. There is nothing very contentious here. The Eight High Trances of Buddhism are as capable of scientific verification as any less dignified psychological or psychic state. The psychological knowledge of the followers of the Dhamma is known to be of a very high standard.

What is contentious is the implication that such methodology, used in an unorthodox fashion – be it legitimate to some school or strictly experimental or even accidental – is capable of throwing a consciousness not too dissimilar to the average Westerner's into a state where an intelligence (be it part of his consciousness or entirely distinct) called 'Aiwass, the minister of Hoor-paar-kraat' could dictate a book as significant to human thought, if not yet to history, as the Bible, yet in a cultural context where such things are either not credited, or are thought to have conveniently ceased in a bygone era. Certainly Crowley did not stagger down from one of his many mountaineering expeditions clutching vitrified stone tablets engraved in letters of heavenly fire. What he did do is scarcely less problematical.

Indeed, the difficulties are of considerably greater scope. Had he produced a 'Book from Eternity' in the fashion of Moses, then only the gullible would have been impressed. Such things are today, after all, within the capability of any man possessing rudimentary skills with a power tool and the gift of the gab. To produce *Liber AL* – a book possessed of such startling mathematical structures – armed only with a fountain pen, is quite another matter.

So, returning to our purpose, we have to obtain a similar degree of familiarity with ecstatic and mystical states and techniques as Crowley, and a philosophical frame of reference such as he possessed. This is what fitted him to be scribe, and will serve us in interpretation. The second point we need to establish is the nature of the relationship between Qaballist and text. Let us examine the procedures of the Kabbalists and their ancient forebears and learn from them what such a relationship entails; this we cannot learn from Crowley or his peers in the Golden Dawn, for their claim to possess any significant portion of the Kabbalah is extremely suspect.

At this point, it is amusing to dilate upon the subject of 'authority' in Kabbalistic matters a little: 'From the brilliant misunderstandings and misrepresentations of... Eliphas Levi, to the highly coloured humbug of Aleister Crowley and his followers, the most eccentric and fantastic statements have been produced purporting to be legitimate interpretations of Kabbalism.' Thus writes Gershom G. Scholem in *Major Trends in Jewish Mysticism*, to which he adds in a footnote: 'No words need to be wasted on the subject of Crowley's "Kabbalistic" writings in his books on what he was pleased to term "Magick", and in his journal, *The Equinox*'. It is worthy of note that Scholem also avoids mentioning the vast majority of Renaissance

'Christian Cabbalists', in whose tradition Crowley and the Golden Dawn possessed more legitimacy.

Crowley was not exactly complimentary about the Hebrew system either: 'The Qabalah, that is the Jewish Tradition concerning the initiated interpretation of their Scriptures, is mostly either unintelligible or nonsense.' (*Little Essays Towards Truth*). Crowley's argument is reasonable enough in context, but once we examine his other works on Kabbalah we find inconsistencies, for while here he is lauding the Tree of Life as an analytic tool in transcendental philosophy, elsewhere he leaps into the 'unintelligible nonsense' in a big way, particularly via gematria, apparently operating a double standard; on rare occasions he even uses colel, surely the most notorious fudge in the repertoire of Hebrew – and, for that matter, Greek – Kabbalists. Our understanding of the relationship of Kabbalist with text is not going to be advanced much by Crowley, since that tradition was virtually a closed book to him.

The modus operandi of traditional Kabbalism is ascertainable from such works as those of Scholem and of Kaplan. Although the former authority is explicitly uncharitable to the work of non-Jewish Kabbalists, and the latter implicitly, this is perhaps readily excused on the grounds of both the cultural heritage and scholastic background of these two authors. Disregarding these limitations, we should look closely into their works for a picture of traditional Kabbalism of greater lucidity than was available in Crowley's day. The main features that emerge are:

A) Extreme immersion in the written word of the Torah, coupled with intense prayer and meditation.

B) The manipulation of words and letters in order to achieve trance and enter spiritual regions with evocative names like 'The Fifty Gates' and 'The Seven Palaces'.

C) Practices roughly analogous to the Grimoires of the Middle Ages and earlier magical practices of greater or lesser antiquity. A telling example of this is the basic analogy between the ascent of the shaman's ladder and the ascent of the Tree of Life.

In terms of Western occultism as nowadays understood, the closest approximation to this procedure is the Abramelin Retirement, with its emphasis on prayer and immersion in the *Holy Books*. The unfamiliar factor is the use of Kabbalistic procedures in this immersion. In most other respects, the magical apparatus surrounding the method is one familiar to all students of the arcane. Given the linguistic, religious and cultural distance between Hebrew Kabbalists and Thelemic magicians, the gravest difficulties existed in accessing or even understanding these elements of Kabbalistic practice. This at least was the case before the discovery of the English Qaballa in November 1976.

We have so far discussed symbolism, language and structure, but dealt only lightly with matters of technique. The reader must not suppose that parroting the many rituals in this handbook will accomplish a great deal without first mastering certain techniques. Symbols have little or no power in themselves; they are channels for power. The internal coherence that a well-developed Qaballa possesses is analogous to the integrity of electrical circuitry, or the compatibility of computer hardware. Certainly Astro-Qaballa provides an undogmatic flexibility of structure which may be turned to any conceivable purpose, but like the electrical circuit, it requires the power to be switched on.

It has been said that all paths lead to the same place, but this is only true insofar as all paths end where they begin, with the Self. Similarly, beyond dogma and beyond symbol, all technique starts at the same place, wherever it may go from there. This place is our Body (including the mind, the chakras, the soul and other subtle conceptualisations of the more mysterious qualities of our physical/psychical being).

In practice this means that while cultural conditioning and other factors influence our interpretation of the experiences obtained through techniques of a magical, tantric or mystical nature, the techniques themselves tend to produce similar experiences. Subtle theological distinctions often become very 'blurred' when comparing accounts of the experiences of meditators from differing religious backgrounds. The unity of religions is not to be sought in a common ideology, for nothing will be found there but a diluted ecumenical morality. The true unity is in the common experience of mystics within distinct traditions, whose practices, beginning as they do with the human constitution, both physical and psychic, lead to similar results.

The best magical systems therefore are generally those that advocate seeking out and learning from whatever sources are available. In our search for workable techniques and frameworks, we require the freedom of belief advocated by Crowley, Spare, Carroll and others. Merely imitating any one of them would be futile; what is required is to employ the method of Contrast. When a particular author's methods and philosophy are attractive then of course we will employ them, but we need to 'balance' this with an equal and opposite involvement with their diametrical opposite.

Radical Modernism requires contrasting with Rampant Traditionalism, and we need to be equally involved with each in its determined place in our work. We must beware of accepting one with unthinking approval and merely going through the motions with the other simply to 'know thine enemy' through role-playing a barely understood stereotype. In particular, be it well understood that there are approaches which suit our preconceptions and temperament, and there are others which do not – following one and neglecting the other is a common (and frequently catastrophic) error. It is a curious psychological fact that the things which repel us often have the most to teach us.

Implicit in this 'Magicians Book' therefore are two principles which form a hidden dynamic in the structure of this book. This bipolar dynamic is the paradoxical interplay of Scepticism and Cultism. Too great a tendency in either direction requires resolute determination to employ the principle of Contrast. The Sceptical magician who employs 'Contrast' will find tremendous power in the devotionalism of Tantra and the religiosity of the Grimoires. The Cultic magician who employs 'Contrast' can only benefit from the

Scientific Illuminism of Thelema and the hard-headed emphasis on technique epitomised by Chaos Magic.

Many contemporary authors have written on the virtues of the Sceptical approach, so that consequently the Sceptical approach has a very positive image. The term 'cult' on the other hand has gained many adverse connotations in the modern world. The true occultist should never permit the abuse of the language by the media to blind them to the true importance of ideas. Ideas despised and devalued in mainstream culture are frequently found to be of cardinal importance in occultism. A magical cult possesses practical virtues which may be obscured by unmerited deference to intellectual fashion. For example, it should be blindingly apparent to those with the courage and ability for magick that Tantra and Voodoo are cults of particular significance to magick, and their very 'cultishness' is the source of much of their power.

PART THREE

We are the most dangerous enemies of our own principles; we alone can betray them, though every other person in the world attempts to cause us to do so, we alone have the power to say yea or nay.

– from *Liber 187*

God's Holy Mysteries

*I ask you to look both ways. For the road to a
knowledge of the stars leads through the atom;
and important knowledge of the atom has been
reached through the stars.*
— Sir Arthur Eddington

In these processes we are dealing with what in Dee's
time would have been called God's Holy Mysteries.
In our own day, we are accustomed to speaking of
archetypes, of constructs, egregores, cones of power or
simply 'synthetic spirits'. The idea that the Universe is
run by (not simply created by) some kind of deity is not
terribly fashionable, and 'does not compute' with our
modern scientific viewpoint, not even for the average
layman, let alone the hard-headed physicist. The use
of the word 'God' or even 'god' is likely to be extremely
contentious, nor am I fool enough or dogmatic enough
to promote an unquestioning belief in superhuman
intelligence. It has become almost an article of faith for
Thelemites to believe in extraterrestrial intelligence,
due to Aleister Crowley and Kenneth Grant et al
insisting that communication with such intelligences
is of supreme importance in magical work. This
is certainly not my attitude — it may be extremely
important at some stage for such communication to
develop, but the question is at which?

In the initial stages of magical work, I believe it is important not to seek such apocalyptic goals. As if having another chapter of *Liber AL* dictated to us would serve any purpose when we don't understand the first three sufficiently well to agree on first principles! What is important, obviously enough, is to train your various faculties – psychic, physical and mental – to the highest possible degree. To accustom yourself to the terminology and methodology of the best occult traditions, and to investigate for yourself their various claims. This must be done in the most thoroughgoing manner possible, with or without an occult order or teacher to assist you.

Train yourself to the highest possible degree of skill and understanding which is within your capability. It is then that such adventures as the Knowledge and Conversation of the Holy Guardian Angel (whatever that may mean) become possible, and meaningful, not before. The career of the noted occultist Frater Achad is a case in point, he undertook incredible magical tasks, and achieved a great deal – but his lack of proper training and preparation led to major flaws in his work, and his personal life and sanity were gravely affected in consequence.

The result of this adventure was that the more significant parts of his work (his Qabalistic key to *The Book of the Law*) have been obscured and tainted by association with his follies. His particular fall was occasioned by prematurely taking the Oath of the Abyss, neglecting the work of several intervening grades. I do not hold up the A.'.A.'. curriculum as an inflexible standard, nor do I wish to impose artificial Masonic inspired hierarchical structures on the aspiring magician.

The point is that while contact with Secret Chiefs, Crossing the Abyss or contacting the Holy Guardian Angel are important and significant objectives (in or out of a grade system as used in the 19th Century), the magician will do well to pursue a balanced course of magical training before attempting any such thing. The length and nature of this training is not for me to delineate, but for the intelligent aspirant to consider carefully for themselves. The A∴A∴ curriculum has much to recommend it despite the problems of the hierarchical structure and the tendency of its modern exponents to freeze magical studies in an antiquated form. Pursued solo or with some sensible guidance there is still an enormous amount of value to be obtained from it.

But even so, what of these Holy Mysteries, and what of God? The answer is, as intimated earlier, that the Qaballa demonstrates that *The Book of the Law* could not have been produced by any human intelligence – in the terms we understand – or by any means which science can as yet begin to comprehend. The mathematical and philosophical complexities revealed by a simple letter-number substitution technique, in which the 'cheats' that are possible with such alphabets as Hebrew are simply not present or possible, make it inconceivable that Crowley or any other occultist of his calibre – let alone someone of lesser ability – could have written it.

The Qaballa reveals a good deal more besides, of an esoteric nature, and on a level so advanced that the training above described is almost essential to even appreciate a portion of it. It is true that processes such as invocation and astrological timing are comparatively simple to put into effect. What is not simple is dealing with the *Book* on its own level, and following the chains of ideas and number symbolism to their ultimate goal. This requires not only considerable intellectual gifts, but also – dare I say it – moral qualities rarely found in twentieth century culture. The very simplest of rules in traditional magick assume phenomenal importance in this area. *The Book of the Law* simply does not envisage, and consequently cannot accommodate, any individual who is not possessed of the traditional qualities of a magician becoming involved with it.

Of primary importance, considering the very nature of the *Book*, is the ability to keep one's word, for one's word to mean what it says. Even with this, there are no guarantees of success in approaching the 'Sovereign Sanctuaries' which its structure reveals and conceals. This indeed is the great secret of its construction, that the elements which reveal its meaning for initiates are the same mechanisms that conceal its secrets from the profane. The last words of *The Book of the Law* are: '*The Book of the Law* is Written and Concealed.' Elsewhere it says: 'it is revealed by Aiwass', and the words CONCEALED and REVEALED have the same numerical value; and this, like each and every turn of phrase and choice of words in the *Book*, is no accident.

'Now let the light devour men and eat them up with blindness' is no idle threat, it is fact; the light which enables us to see is the very instrument by which *AL* blinds us to its truths – blinds us, that is, until or unless we are ready. We must approach *AL* with great courage and determination, this much it tells us itself; we must also approach it with knowledge and humility, with great sincerity and humanity – that much it simply assumes, for it was not written for persons devoid of these qualities. Such individuals it will puff up with pride and lead to their destruction. Modern fairy tales such as *Raiders of the Lost Ark* portray extremely graphically the consequences of seeking to pervert the energies of such 'sacred' power sources.

There is no question of such consequences being 'unfair', nor of calling the sanctity of the *Book* into question on the basis of such events. It would be most unwise to make such judgements. It has been said that magical energy is neutral, and that it is men who turn it to one end or another, in a similar manner to electricity. This analogy is only partially helpful here. Certainly, those who tap these energies without due preparation have only themselves to blame for undesirable results, but the energy is not neutral. It has a viewpoint, it has a purpose, and it is the attempt to manipulate it or deal with it in terms alien to its nature which produces such dire results. *AL* makes it quite clear that these consequences exist, and that attempts to use it without understanding are dangerous. It is unfortunate if these warnings go unheeded, but it is not 'unfair'.

What then is the purpose of the *Book?* The answer here is simple, in that it can be expressed in one word, and complex, in that this word involves imponderables beyond human comprehension. The purpose is, in one word: Initiation. Initiation of the individual, of the collective and of the human species. The individual is the primary concern of the *Book* at this time. This is because the individual is the logical beginning for the entire process – logical in *AL*'s own terms of reference. That the ultimate purpose of *AL* is to initiate a new phase in human evolution is, perhaps, a commonplace; nevertheless, a discussion of this kind cannot omit to mention it.

The immediate form of initiation which the Qaballa of *AL* has made possible is through the Sun-Venus Pentagram. This is initiation by ordeal, the Ordeal X described cryptically in *The Book of the Law*. This Ordeal separates the chaff from the wheat, the fit from the unfit. What it does not do is make silk purses out of sows' ears. This said, there is abundant evidence that the Ordeal initiates persons possessing basic human qualities, regardless of their supposed intelligence or knowledge, or any other supposedly desirable quality. To clarify this, I must resort to biography:

A simple man, a man of no special intelligence, but having real skills in mechanics, such as welding and car maintenance, became involved with a magical order. After a period of time in which he underwent the initiation rituals associated with the Sun-Venus, triggering the Ordeal X, a transformation occurred in his make-up. His former skills were not lessened; indeed if anything they were greatly enhanced, and he made some of the most impressive ritual weapons it has been my privilege to see. Yet this was not the most striking transformation. The same individual became an extremely competent astrologer – not in itself that remarkable in an astrologically oriented group, had he not also developed excellent skills as a counsellor, a rare gift, especially with no formal training. This was by no means all; the same individual, within a period of about three years, had acquired all these abilities, undergone a major personality transformation (a clear-out of conditioning inherited from society) and without any peer-group pressure whatsoever (as might be inferred in the case of astrological skills) had developed remarkable psychometric gifts, with a degree of sensitivity usually associated with women of an otherwise frail constitution and unworldly temperament. These transformations in his personality and make-up, involving such varied skills and abilities, were all accomplished without his 'losing the common touch'.

His abilities with metals were obviously not diminished, nor was his ability to mix and work with the same social group he always had previously, but nor was he out of his depth among the initiates of the Order. Of course, this man was not a 'sow's ear' to begin with, else he would never have been involved with this group in the first place, and supposing he had, would have been swiftly ejected from the system by the mechanical processes of the Ordeal itself. This case history has a particular point to it, in terms of the almost religious nature of the Qaballistic path – it indicates that the Ordeal X and the system of magical initiation associated with it possess a moral dimension; that, as a great magician of another tradition once remarked, a handful of moral qualities are worth a hundred magical powers.

As a Qaballist I would say this is true, but also that these same qualities are great magical powers. If we take a look at the names of the Sephiroth they seem archaic and alien. If, however, we look more closely, reminding ourselves what these titles mean in our own language, we become aware of something we might not have noted consciously before. Let us do as I suggest, and examine these titles in English, not as gematria values, but as simple words: The Crown; Wisdom; Understanding; Knowledge; Mercy or Glory; Justice or Power; Beauty, Harmony or Compassion; Victory; Splendour; The Foundation, and finally, The Kingdom.

These are moral powers, human qualities and ideals. If we imagine for a moment that the Hebrew Kabbalah and indeed all previous systems are abrogate, that the magick of the future retains the essence but not the outward forms, then the Tree of Life in our time might have other qualities, of a similar nature, rather than this list. If we look back to the origins of the Kabbalah, we find that such lists have existed before. The 'pre-Kabbalistic' sage Rav, of the third century AD, said: 'Ten are the qualities with which the world has been created: Wisdom, Insight, Knowledge, Force, Appeal, Power, Justice, Right, Love and Compassion.' In our own times, it might be that the Universe is interpreted in terms of the qualities of Liberty, Truth, Justice, Courage, Integrity, Love, Reverence, Strength, Conscience, Pleasure and Serenity, or any number of similar qualities. This idea might become the centre of an important meditative practice.

Another important point that arises is the difficulty we have in seeing what is under our noses. Many students of the Kabbalah fail to recognise that the Sephiroth are moral powers; they see the exotic titles rather than the meaning, nor is this entirely their own fault. If nothing else, EQ brings home to its devotees the interior world of the Qaballa. To the Hebrews these old titles were not exotic, the words struck home to them just as the word 'freedom' sounds in the ear of an oppressed person in the land of a tyrant, or 'love' in the ear of a young girl. In the same way, the English Qaballa brings us the power and potency of the ancient magick in a form comprehensible to the aspirants and adepts of today.

To return to our theme, of course the ability to produce wonderful effects is what we expect from a magician, or indeed from ourselves as magicians – at least once in a while. This is only too understandable (we are all children after all in many ways), but we know too that the ability to love, to understand or to behave honourably is also miraculous, and is worthy of a magician, or even a saint. These are all magical powers, and will move mountains as effectively as any lightning bolts from the fingertips, or ectoplasmic strands from the mouth and nostrils.

When we speak of Archetypal forces, what are we really talking about? Not some strange dreamlike character such as the Jungian Animus, nor any god, spirit or hobgoblin. An Archetypal force is a human or universal quality such as Justice, and any person who personifies such a force possesses magical power. This reminds me of the Golden Dawn motto, 'Strive to become more than human'; this is altogether too ridiculous, for without at least one or two of these qualities (dormant or half-forgotten) in our hearts or minds, we are not even human, let alone more than human!

Possessing one of these powers is not easy. We are the most dangerous enemies of our own principles; we alone can betray them, though every other person in the world attempts to cause us to do so, we alone have the power to say yea or nay. There, I've done it, I've bitten the bullet and talked as straight as I can on the single most important aspect of Initiation, the candidate and their ordeal. Of course, this will leave you none the wiser should you undertake the adventure, for Initiation is never what you expect, or it would not be Initiation. I have risked making myself ridiculous, by pontificating at such extravagant length, and though it is time to turn to magical procedures, to meditation, to practical Qaballa, do not lose sight of what has passed between us in these few pages. Magical power is real, more real than any other form of power, and yet more subtle and illusive.

PRACTICAL QABALLA TODAY

"Only the one who does not question is safe
from making a mistake."

– Albert Einstein

THE TABLES OF A.M.E.N.

THESE TABLES ARE DESIGNED TO FACILITATE THE construction of rituals on qaballistic lines, and have been used with great success by several groups and individuals for some years. The cosmology implicit in this schema originated with empirical work with EQ and astrological ritual. It is important to bear in mind that this model is part of a greater system, and that the system in question has a 'slant' or emphasis on particular regions of experience. While the general symbolism is essentially similar to astrology and even pre-existent qaballistic models, the resemblance is superficial. Accordingly, we find such apparent anomalies as PLUTO = 76 = TAURUS, ARIES = 66 = URANUS = EARTH, and CANCER = 78 = FIRE. In the region in which EQ lives and moves and has its being, these 'anomalies' become potent arcanum.

The foregoing remarks must serve as sufficient warning that this attribution concerns realms distinct from or tangential to those the conventional astrologer or ceremonialist is concerned with. In a word, EQ has 'attitude'. The emphasis is, to most practical intents, on the movement of the planets and luminaries through four signs of the zodiac. Where other signs are concerned, they must be understood in terms of this emphasis. Accordingly, while astrological expertise is a definite advantage, astrological dogma may be entirely counterproductive; EQ does not much care that Aries begins the year, or that Cancer is associated with the home or parents. It is concerned with forms of initiation and experience outside of the conventional occultism of virtually any era; a truly 'New Aeon' system, of 'new symbols'.

The first of these symbols, of course, is ONE (since Zero or NONE 'precedes the beginning') and in EQ ONE has the value 46. Of all the words in AL with this value, the most significant and fundamental idea is WOMAN. But of Her we do not speak – which plays a part in the construction of the Tables of A.M.E.N..

The tables which follow divide the universe into Four Worlds – a conventional pattern so far. (There is another sense in which it appears that Thelemic Qabalism posits Three Worlds, but that need not concern us here.) The Four Scales of Number representing these Worlds are, for recondite reasons, given as headings the four letters of the Word or Name AMEN.

The first of these scales represents the 'Infinite' or highest expression of the idea concerned; in the case of ideas classified under 5, the highest or infinite expression is taken to be 58 (using 8 for Infinity), for 10, 108, and so on. Names corresponding to these values have been placed in the columns as appropriate on numerical grounds. The second such scale represents a more materialised or extended form of the original idea. Now the number is spelt, so that 5 = FIVE = 76, and so this column consists of Names equivalent to the gematrias of the numbers. The third column, corresponding to Vau or the Son in Hebrew symbolism, is a combination of the two preceding, its father and mother, as it were.

Staying with the number five as our example, this means that in the third column the Name will be equivalent to 5 + FIVE which is 81, the value of KHEPHRA among other Names, which will be found accordingly in that place in the table. The fourth column represents the formal symbol in the macrocosm of the number in question. Although other forms of symbolism are entirely possible here, the beginner is warned against any personalised attribution, for should these be incompatible with the true nature of the force, the results will be at best disappointing and at worst catastrophic. The best course is to use the conventional planets and elements, bearing in mind the nature of the system itself in relation to those symbols. To EQ, Fire is a symbol of the Goddess, since FIRE = 78 = NUIT. So whilst it is conventional to attribute both Venus and Fire to the number Seven (Hebrew Netzach, representing the Elemental grade of Fire and the Planet Venus), it is worthy of particular note that in EQ VENUS = 71 and FIRE = 78, as if to ram some special point home.

One further point before turning to the Tables themselves: it might appear logical from the view of mathematics that the series should start with ONE, but in practice, which is the whole purpose of these Tables, the number ONE as a symbol of WOMAN is concealed ('Let them speak not of Thee as One'), so the series begins with the number twelve in the place of one, and continues through to eleven.

The Thelemite with a close relationship with the *Holy Books of Thelema* will also recall this passage from Liber Ararita: '...he tried ever his work by the Star 418. And it deceived him not; for by his subtlety he expanded it all into the Twelve Rays of the Crown. And these twelve rays were One'. In this way when EQ departs from the forms of older models it will be found that these departures have also been 'tried by the Star 418' and are anticipated in the Class A material. In any case this arrangement has proved far more satisfactory in all ways than the first option, and is undoubtedly the correct form.

	A. INFINITE	M. NUMBER	E. SERPENT	N. SYMBOL
TWELVE	128. Baphomet	89. Nu-Ha-It	101. Mentu	76. (Pluto) Heru-Ra-Ha
TWO	28. Ankh	34. Al Oai Abra	Aiwaz Amn	145. (Neptune) Asi-Nepthi
THREE	38. Aiwass Yama	90. Typhon	93. Tahuti	73. (Saturn) (Ra-Hoo-Khu)
FOUR	48. Asar-Isa	54. Set Buddha	58. Hadit	143. (Jupiter) Sol Invictus
FIVE	58. Heru	76. Heru-Ra-Ha	81. Kephra Tanech	39. (Mars) Aum
SIX	68. Jesus	50. Bes Coph	56. Isis Khonsu	36. (Sun) Aiwaz
SEVEN	78. Nuit	79. Abrahadabra	86. Titan	71. (Venus) Io Pan
EIGHT	88. Coph Nia	87. Falutli	96. Aormuzdi	115. (Mercury) Nu%Had*
NINE	98. Qadosh-Isis	76. Iacchus	86. Shosinel	49. (Moon) Mary Eros
TEN	98. Hoor-Apep	63. Maut	73. Bacchus	66. (Earth) E.I.A.T.
ELEVEN	118. Ankh-Af-Na-Khnosu	101. Mentu	112. Isis-Isis	66. (Uranus) E.I.A.T.

*These two Names must be 'counted well' to obtain this value. This technique has proved time and again to be of value in ritual, whilst apparently being an obscure qaballistic method. It is for this reason that it is described 'longhand' in early issues of *The Equinox:BJoT*, despite the fact that a quicker and simpler method exists.

The vast majority of these Names are from Class A. One or two are combinations, and in the case of SOL INVICTUS the form was simply too apt to ignore. The Name SHOSINEL is an anagram of the word Holiness, the literal meaning of QADOSH. Of the combined Names, it is worth remarking that ISIS-HATHOR is named with reverence in *Liber 418*, whilst HOOR-APEP is a principal form in *Liber Pyramidos* and elsewhere.

The point to be borne in mind is that it is the number rather than the letters which give this table its chief efficacy; in theory one could construct completely synthetic names to match these values. The student must find by experiment how best to apply these tables.

In the many kinds of ritual work including invocation, evocation and talismans, etc., and in the equally various meditative and trance induction techniques in which Barbarous Names or Words are useful, there are often subtle qualitative distinctions to be made which are derived both from the general psychic reality underlying the practice and the particular psyche of the individual operator. Taking the numbers rather than the particular names given here as their guide, the student must research and vary their practice accordingly. It may be that in talismanic magick and formal ceremonial they find the use of recognisable Names to be the most potent, while in mantra or meditative work devised or 'received' names or words of equivalent value are found to be more effective, or vice versa. In many cases it appears to be the work done by the student in preparing themselves and the 'rubric' of the ritual that renders particular forms most effective.

What should be carefully avoided is thinking of, say, Nuit as a Spirit of Fire, or of Iacchus as a Moon-God. Whilst some such associations are valid within limits – such as Jesus' association with the Sun in 'Christian' Qabalah – the tendency if unchecked would wreck the system rather than access it fully.

The important thing is that Magical Names have POWER and through their numerical values that power may be used to control or to access specific energies of the Universe. That this is literally true may come as somewhat of a shock, and the reader may choose to disbelieve it. In the context of an astrologically timed tantric ritual, however, every word and action is significant – it is important in such circumstances to say and do only what you intend. The effect of such words and actions in the context of such a ritual are enormously increased compared to the day-to-day effect of willed/unwilled and half-intentional words and actions, given the confused and uncertain manner in which human interaction with the environment is generally conducted.

Proceeding with the Table in the Sphere of the Elements, the ritualist alters the fourth column in lines 6 through to 10 as follows:

(6)   68.   50.   56. 113/Spirit   = Ra-Hrumachis

(7)   78.   79.   86. 78/Fire   = Apep

(8)   88.   87.   95. 65/Water   = Babalon

(9)   98.   76.   85. 36/Air   = Aiwaz

(10)   108.   63.   73. 66/Earth   = Fiat

These Names are used to formulate the Pentagrams or AL sigils in the Four Quarters in the Pentagram Rites, Opening Rituals etc. in use by the groups and individuals mentioned earlier. Examples of specially crafted forms of this ritual follow in their place within this book.

THE TREES OF ETERNITY

4. I worship the Devi of all Devis, the great Shri
Siddha Matrika, whose letters of the alphabet,
like moonlight, adorn the three worlds.
Vamakeshvara Tantra

THE THEORY OF MAGICK IN THIS BOOK IS BASED ON THE IDEA
that the Universe is a self contained system, which will,
when left to its own devices, produce a standard reality
where Free Will is limited and patterns are fairly
stable, going round and round in circles. Fortunately
this circular system is periodically interrupted by
a flow of energy between the manifest universe and
another 'perfect' universe.

Golden Dawn Qabalists used to have a Tree of
Life based on the Garden of Eden before the Fall and
another Tree of Life representing the state of affairs
after the Fall. Behind the biblical language of this
conception lurks a profound magical truth.

Kenneth Grant, among others, speculated on a
'Two Trees' system, others of a 'top to bottom' Tree
versus a 'bottom to top' one, i.e. same Tree, different
point of view. The English Qaballa takes this idea of
Two Trees to express the theoretical basis of Thelemic
magick. While the qaballistic calculations involved
are complex, the idea is very simple.

There is a manifest Universe and an unmanifest Universe, a Tree of Manifestation and a Tree of Hadit. The interplay between the two is both periodic and constant, and can be manipulated to produce change in accordance with will. This energy we call the 93 Current; it interrupts the play of 'conventional' forces with results which can be disruptive and destructive of existing orders. This need not be an antisocial or cataclysmic intervention. If the 'status quo' is a dry, unproductive phase in the life of the magician then invoking 93, as Crowley and others have expressed it, is to induce a new current, a fresh inspiration beating the doldrums. On the other hand its capacity to produce change can be applied in several spheres, and some are capable of producing enormous transformations in the seemingly stable world about us.

There are many ways of invoking the 93 Current, and this theory embraces all of them. Of particular interest are the two spheres of human physiology and of astrological timing. There are precise analogies between the female reproductive cycle and the zodiacal cycle, in particular the Scorpio Current is linked to menstruation. There are lunar 93 periods, and there are planetary aspects which are also appropriate for Thelemic magick as defined here. There is a constant as well as a periodic interplay of the Trees of Eternity, so that while some times are particularly powerful for specific purposes, 'there are means and means'. There is always 'help and hope in other spells' as *The Book of the Law* expresses it; when the astrological universe is being unhelpful and producing only more of the same, the magician should not be without resource. On the other hand the magician who is unable to harness astrological forces when they are in his favour is at a great disadvantage, and the EQ has been of great assistance in reconstructing the principles of magical astrology, a task which beat Crowley and Mathers.

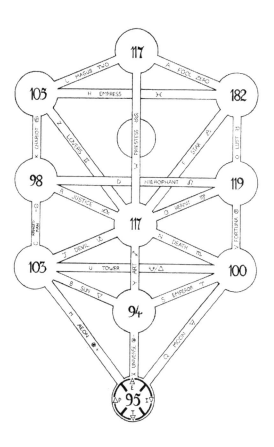

THE TREE OF MANIFESTATION

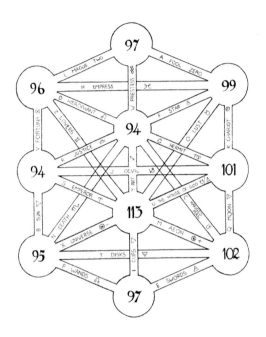

THE TREE OF HADIT

MAGICK SQUARES

THERE ARE MANY KINDS OF MAGICK SQUARE – INCLUDING rectangles and even diamonds under that generic title – and the form has a very ancient history, being found in Chinese, Arab and Nordic occultism as well as the more widely known 'Western Tradition' of Judaeo-Christian occultism, itself derived from Hellenistic Greek originals. Although these grids, whether square or not, frequently contain numbers, this is by no means always the case; 'squares' composed of letters and sigil-like characters are often encountered in occult research.

Moreover, when numbers are used they are not necessarily a consecutive series; the same number may occur more than once and no strict sequence may exist. Dee's tablets are a species of magick square, and quite apart from the Tablet of Union and the four Elemental tablets there is a huge class of such squares in the writings of Dee, some if not most of which are of rectangular form, as indeed are the five above mentioned, for each elemental tablet is 12 by 13, while the Tablet of Union is 4 by 5.

The age and complexity of these 'squares' has created many problems for occultists and researchers alike. Even the best known class, to which the 'planetary squares' belong, are seldom understood or used correctly. I was fortunate enough to learn the practical magical applications of this class of magick squares early in my magical career. Strangely enough I learnt it not from a heretical rabbi but from Paul Huson's under-rated classic of eclectic witchcraft, *Mastering Witchcraft*.

Quite simply, when drawing one of the squares of the planets in ritual, write the numbers **in numerical order**. In this way several purposes are served; an auto-hypnotic state is induced, the principal sigil form associated with the square is traced by the numerical sequence, so that in writing the numbers in order you have traced the sigil, and the entire process has attuned you to the energies represented by the square. As Huson expresses it, you have dialled the number of the forces invoked. The pattern thus traced does not always conform to the traditional sigil, but is undoubtedly the master pattern of the square, and thus of more use.

Simply copying the square with no attention to the principles of construction achieves nothing but a copy, no force is awakened, and no higher state than a degree of concentration on a monotonous task is achieved. The existence of several other classes of square means of course that more than one technique is involved, but the induction of a directed trance is a feature of the entire genre.

An important attribution of larger squares in the same class as these 'planetary squares' is to be found in the writings of the Qaballist Joseph Tzyach (1505-1573), discussed in some depth in Kaplan's *Meditation and Kabbalah*. Tzyach attributes the seven planetary squares in the traditional manner, but does not extend this attribution to the Sephiroth associated with those planets. Instead he attributes a square of ten to Kether, eleven to Chokmah, twelve to Binah, thirteen to Chesed and fourteen to Geburah, then a break at fifteen (the Abyss?), recommencing at sixteen for Tiphereth and thence on without further breaks to twenty for Malkuth.

An important feature of this is the attribution of Chesed to the thirteen-fold square. A square 13 by 13 appears as the first plate in *Liber 963: The Treasure House of Images*, followed on the facing page by an arrangement of the Sephiroth and the Three Veils of the Negative into a Tau Cross surrounded by yonis, a diagram students may recognise as the basis of the design of Crowley's Magick Circle.

93	108	123	138	153	168	1	16	31	46	61	76	91
107	122	137	152	167	13	15	30	45	60	75	90	92
121	136	151	166	12	14	29	44	59	74	89	104	106
135	150	165	11	26	28	43	58	73	88	103	105	120
149	164	10	25	27	42	57	72	87	102	117	119	134
163	9	24	39	41	56	71	86	101	116	118	133	148
8	23	38	40	55	70	85	100	115	130	132	147	162
22	37	52	54	69	84	99	114	129	131	146	161	7
36	51	53	68	83	98	113	128	143	145	160	6	21
50	65	67	82	97	112	127	142	144	159	5	20	35
64	66	81	96	111	126	141	156	158	4	19	34	49
78	80	95	110	125	140	155	157	3	18	33	48	63
79	94	109	124	139	154	169	2	17	32	47	62	77

The square, unlike the other diagram, receives no commentary or elucidation. Tzyach's attribution is therefore of interest, since Chesed is associated with the Hebrew God-name AL value 31, and 13, 31 and 131 are significant numbers in Thelemic Qaballa, both pre and post 1976. 963 is an important document, built entirely on a thirteen-fold structure, while thirteen is half of twenty six, the value of the Spheres of the Middle Pillar, of the Name Yod-He-Vau-He in Hebrew, and the number of the letters of the English alphabet.

Returning to our techniques, we have shown how the traditional squares of the planets and others of their class may be used. This technique applies, whether or not we write the numbers upon the basic grid. For example, the Name BABALON has seven letters, and She is associated with Venus (for the significance of the Sun-Venus in Thelema even before the discovery of EQ see the *Vision and the Voice: A Comment upon the Nature of the Aethyrs*, particularly Aethyrs 25 and 24) and accordingly a square of Venus may be used in invoking Her.

A variety of methods are possible. Firstly there is the simple technique outlined above, simply writing the numbers in sequence (appropriate coloured or scented inks may be used to strengthen the link) but, since Babalon is not to be confused with the more 'traditional' conceptions of Venus it might be better to construct a square exclusive to Her. Accordingly we may write Her Name seven times in the square, writing the letters in the numerical order of the square of Venus:

B	A	B	A	L	O	N	22	47	16	41	10	35	4
N	B	A	B	A	L	O	5	23	48	17	42	11	29
O	N	B	A	B	A	L	30	6	24	49	18	36	12
L	O	N	B	A	B	A	13	31	7	25	43	19	37
A	L	O	N	B	A	B	38	14	32	1	26	44	20
B	A	L	O	N	B	A	21	39	8	33	2	27	45
A	B	A	L	O	N	B	46	15	40	9	34	3	28

As the order of the numerical sequence of the square of Venus determines which letter is written first and where, this method retains the benefits of the sigil tracing and attuning methods without diminishing Babalon to the status of a Venusian 'spirit' like Hagiel. A curious effect of this type of square is that the order of numbers in odd numbered squares follows the diagonals, and through interaction with the diagonals of the word-grid this means our first seven letters will be N, the second seven L and so on.

Alternatively we can use the technique known as 'counting well', where every letter of one word (a) is added to every letter of another word (b), filling a grid whose width is determined by the number of letters in word (a) and whose depth is determined similarly with reference to word (b). This is the longhand form of this calculation, which briefly is value of word (a) times number of letters in word (b) and vice versa. Both the long-hand and short-hand versions of this seemingly abstruse method have practical ritual applications, and a little familiarisation with them will reveal that the complexity is only apparent, and their applications are very direct and simple to put into operation.

Should we decide to use this technique then Babalon is both word a) and word b) and the gematria result is 910: 91 is the sum of the numbers one to thirteen, and of seven multiplied by thirteen, and has considerable significance in Qabalism ancient and modern. Interestingly also, the value of Babalon in Crowley's 'Hebrew' spelling of her name is 156, connecting her Name to Dee's Enochian Tablets; Her name in English Qaballa is 65, if we add 91 to 65 we obtain 156. Interestingly enough this is also the combined value of the astrological signs attributed to Isis and Nepthys, VIRGO + SCORPIO = 63 + 93 = 156. Moreover the initials of Virgo and Scorpio are readily combined into the traditional symbol of Capricorn.

One of the conventions of English Qaballa occasionally met with in this book analyses the number 156 as The Unity (1) of the Pentagram (5, the Sun-Venus Pentagram is meant here) is the Law (LAW = 6). Key phrases of this value are: THE LOVELY STAR, THESE RUNES, STAR SPLENDOUR, POWER GIVEN, GENETRIX, ABSOLUTE BLISS, IT SHALL NOT FADE. It is also the value of WAND + CUP + SWORD + DISK, and among many other significant Class A values we find: A THUNDERBOLT.

In writing this square we do not need to observe the order of the planetary square, simply calculating the value B + B, B + A, B + B, B + A, B + L, B + O and B + N and writing the result of each calculation in the seven squares of the first column, then A + B, A + A and so on in the next six. This serves as an even more potent attunement technique, has a significant and appropriate gematria value, uses a seven by seven grid, etc. Perhaps we do not need to point out that since Babalon is the Scarlet Woman the usual colour correspondences and etc. do not necessarily apply.

40.	21.	40.	21.	22.	27.	34.
21.	2.	21.	2.	3.	8.	15.
40.	21.	40.	21.	22.	27.	34.
21.	2.	21.	2.	3.	8.	15.
22.	3.	22.	3.	4.	9.	16.
27.	8.	27.	8.	9.	14.	21.
34.	15.	34.	15.	16.	21.	28.

This technique has additional benefits, some of an extremely esoteric nature and others purely practical. One chief practical advantage is that a square or grid obtained by the 'count well' technique will also produce a series of barbarous words for use in rituals involving that particular square. This application is detailed in a later chapter dealing with incantation. The esoteric benefits are concerned with initiation; the closest analogy with the Hebrew system is in the core Kabbalistic techniques known as 'Permutation' and 'The Fifty Gates'.

These techniques were almost entirely omitted from (and inoperable within) the Golden Dawn synthesis. That it could regenerate these methods without compromise with old-aeon forms, and in a completely distinct language is one of the more striking achievements of EQ. The technique of permutation in Hebrew is extremely difficult for non-Hebrews to access due to its reliance on the vowel points, the Hebrew scriptures and a Hebrew/Aramaic vocabulary. Unfortunately it is also one of the most important aspects of the system, so that its loss to the 19th century revival was a serious one. By its means the adept enters the first of the Fifty Gates on a journey that takes him across the Abyss.

The ancient Kabbalists used permutation of letters as a means of a) inducing trance and b) deriving mantras, names, etc. for magical use. The English Qaballa supplies a superior technique to the 'Tables of Permutation' used by the Hebrews et al. The Wakanaba method supplies a means of rendering the permutations pronounceable by allocation of vowels. Supposing that we are using the counting well process to permutate the letters of a word or name, the process will require that our chosen word is counted well either with itself (for example, BABALON counted well with BABALON) or with some other word (for example BABALON counted well with BEAST) each horizontal line of our square thus represents a permutation of the original word, thus the first line of BABALON counted well with BABALON would give, in numerical form:

	B	A	B	A	L	O	N
B:	40	21	40	21	22	27	34

Converting these numbers into sounds by the Wakanaba method becomes:

HOOL MO HOOL MO XU LAOL WAHO

Our first line of numbers is converted into pronounceable syllables and chanted mantra-like, and the combined values of the line may be used to generate the first permutation of the name thus:

$$40+21+40+21+22+27+34 = 205 = LOS = LAOLSU$$

The Qaballist goes on to count well the second line:

21 2 21 2 3 8 15 which converts to
MO LA MO LA WA ZE YO

If desired then add this second line's values, obtaining 75 or OLSU, chanting the results as before, and so on for lines 3 to 7 (the third and fourth line will obviously be identical with lines 1 and 2).

This technique is superior to its forebears for various reasons, not least of which is the Idea the magician is working with generates its own specific 'Table of Permutations' rather than a purely synthetic 'general use' Table with fixed attributions.

It is also superior in that it enables the technique to be used by non-Hebrew-speaking, non-Judaeo-Christian magicians. Although, having permutated a particular set of numbers and words we can then make a note of the names and spells thus obtained for future use, the directed trance induction produced by the initial construction can be accessed again simply by reconstructing the same square on a later subsequent occasion, should it be appropriate to a later operation.

Such squares may be employed in a variety of ways in a ritual context aside from the construction of names and incantations. For example, the qaballistic magician can place a numerical square on the altar in a ritual. At the appropriate point in the ceremony the magician, with a little mental effort, converts each number from memory into their appropriate sounds. In a square composed of letters much the same process applies: each letter is extended, from memory, into its Wakanaba equivalent. In each case the effort of memory and the process of the mantric chant occupy the conscious mind, preventing its interference, while the nature and structure of the square direct the magical current of the ritual to the intended destination via the subconscious.

There are many possible refinements on this technique, and it may be applied alongside many other methods. The planetary squares are excellent adjuncts to invocation, as indeed are 'purpose built' squares. The use of large, lettered squares in particular have a most admirable effect when employed for such purposes. The capacity of such 'qaballistic mantras' to induce trance, in conjunction with appropriate ritual, can be a useful adjunct to ritual divination and sigil magick, or serve as a species of meditation. In talismanic use of these squares the resourceful sorcerer may find it helpful, for practical or purely aesthetic reasons, to devise sigil forms for the numerical range 2 to 52 for use on these squares, in which case some of the material in our chapter on Incantation may be helpful.

A species of magick square not covered so far is the 'revealed' type, obtained through trance, vision or other similar means. An example of this type is the ALSOTH square built on the pattern of 'The Holy 42-fold Table' shown below. This square generates sigils for the 'Secret Chief' AMALANTRAH and for BAPHOMET.

A	L	S	O	T	H
E	M	A	N	T	R
A	S	A	N	D	S
P	E	L	L	S	T
H	E	O	B	E	A
H	A	N	D	T	H
E	W	A	N	G	A

The final Thelemic usage of magick squares in this chapter concerns the infamous 666. This is the total value of the square of the Sun – the fourth number of the Sun in fact: 6 is the first, 36 the second, 111 the third, the square is six by six, thus 36, its columns add to 111, etc. The verse of Revelations which refers to this number has led to some diverse speculations, some better informed than others. For instance, the Gnostic-baiting bishop Iranaeus speculated that 666 referred to some principal pagan god whose name has this value (as Abrasax = 365 etc.). His idea was that this name was TEITAN in Greek characters. In English however the six lettered name TEITAN has the value of 111; accordingly it can be written in the magick square of the Sun in the same way as Babalon in the square of Venus, with the important difference that this square will have the original value of the Square of the Sun, and its individual columns will have the value of the original squares columns. This is a potent Thelemic talisman of the solar-phallic force. (The word SUN counted well with MIDNIGHT also gives this value, See Ritual B2 in *Liber ABA*, and the last few verses of *AL* III).

T	E	I	T	A	N
N	T	E	I	T	A
A	N	T	E	I	T
T	A	N	T	E	I
I	T	A	N	T	E
E	I	T	A	N	T

INTRODUCING THE WAKANABA
KAMEA EXTRAPOLATOR

The following material is the result of the author's anal retentive involvement with magick squares, barbarous tongues and other peculiarities of the Grimoire Tradition. The results are spectacular in many ways, not least being the ease of pronunciation of the barbarous language which results from the technique, and the inexhaustible quantity of 'custom derived' words, and indeed entire incantations, which may be obtained with the minimum of industry by the magician or sorcerer who is stumped for a really mean and utterly original incantation for every conceivable occasion.

The Wakanaba Kamea Extrapolator is a refinement on the magick squares derived from the Counting Well technique (see page 37) used in English Qaballa to combine words and obtain values in the higher ranges of the numerical series. In simple maths this consists of the formula 'value of word A times number of letters in word B' and vice versa. Thus, using the EQ values of the English Alphabet, if the process of counting well is represented by % we can write:

AZURE % LIDDED = 718,
MIDNIGHT % SUN = 666,
ABRA % HADABRA = 418.

The simple math technique outlined above represents the slower process of forming a grid, with word A written across the top, word B written down the side, and the value of the letter combinations written in the appropriate sub-squares of our Magick Square, or if the words be unequal in length, Magick Rectangle!

The Kamea Extrapolator is designed to turn each sub-square into a syllable, and applying simple rules these are combined into lines of an incantation; the same process can then be applied to the value of each column to provide the second 'verse' of the incantation, and the value of the entire square into a Grand Word or Name which is placed at the end of each verse.

The method is as follows: every number in a magick square represents either a letter in the range 1 to 26, or in the case of higher numbers, a combination of letters. These letters are then rendered pronounceable by the simple device of supplying every consonant but L with a vowel, on the following pattern:

W K N B receive an A, (thus "WAKANABA")
H V Y M receive an O,
S G J X receive an U,
D R F T receive an I,
Z C Q P receive an E.

Whenever a number equivalent to a vowel occurs (i.e. 7 = O etc.) it is given an L, thus O = OL. When the number 2 appears (either by itself, or as part of a number higher than 26) it becomes LA. There is a further optional rule whereby double numbers are halved, i.e. 44 becomes HO not HO-HO; this may not hold good for the column values which as we will see produce altogether different words, though retaining the virtue of easy pronunciation.

The final rule is that zero when it appears in numbers higher than 26 is treated as if a 7, for fairly obvious reasons. An example of the entire technique follows. The square was derived from the words BLACK/STONE counted well together. The use to which this may be put is determined in this case by the numerical value 600, interpreted as extending the Law (LAW = 6) into the Three Worlds (three digit number). So having ascertained the purpose of the rite, we can go on from the talismanic square to the qaballistic incantation:

25 44 27 34 45 = EL HE LE WA-HO HO-SU
7 26 9 16 27 = OL PE KA JU LO
6 25 8 15 26 = DI EL ZE YU PE
18 37 20 27 38 = FI WO BA LO WAZE
14 33 16 23 34 = NA WA JU IL WA-HO

70 165 80 115 170 gives us OLOL ALDISU ZE-OL ALALSU ALOLOL.

600 provides us with the Great Word: DIOL-OL.

Rationalising these expressions to personal taste, we would end up with an incantation as follows:

a) ELHOLO WAHO HOSU, OLPEKA JULO, DI ELZE YUPE! FI-WO BALOWAZE; NAWA JUILWA-HO!: DIOL-OL!

b) OL-OL ALDISU ZE-OL ALALSU ALOL-OL: DIOL-OL!

How to Make an EQ Magick Square

Using EQ values a magick square (or grid) may be constructed from any two words by adding the values in the appropriate sub square:

	A	U	M
H	5	21	25
A	2	18	22

Methods of deriving chants and sigils from these squares sound complex, but with a little practice are quite simple.

5=S 21=M 25=E 2=L 18=F 22=X

These letters/numbers may be converted into sounds using the following table and some simple rules:

A.	W	K	N	B
O.	H	V	Y	M
U.	S	G	J	X
I.	D	R	F	T
E.	Z	C	Q	P

S becomes SU
M becomes MO
E becomes EL (vowels from a square are always paired with L)
L becomes LA (L from the square is always paired with A)
F becomes FI
X becomes XU

So we get:

SU MO EL
LA FI XU

The totals of the columns provide an additional part of a spell or chant:

	A	U	M
H	5	21	25
A	2	18	22
	7	39	47

OL WAKA HO-OL

The total of the square provides a 'Grand Word' or 'Name': 7+39+47=93 = KAWA

With a little personalised input our complete spell may be expressed thus:

Sumoel Lafixu: Kawa!
Olwaka Ho, Ol: Kawa!

Alternative methods taking the values and finding Class A Godnames of the same value may be used, or combined with the above, so we might go with:

Sumoel Lafixu Tahuti,
O Aum Maat, Tahuti.

How to construct an EQ Sigil

Blank out sub-squares which contain 7 or 8 or end in 0, 7 or 8 (three forms of Nothing):

- where the number ends in 1 replace it with a line
- where the number is 2 or ends in 2 replace it with a line
- where the number is 3 or ends in 3 replace it with a double curl (like a three, but turned in any direction)
- where the number is 4 or ends in 4 replace it with a cross
- where the number is 5 or ends in 5 replace it with a hook
- where the number is 6 or ends in 6 replace it with a circle, loop or looped line (similar to a six, looped to the right)
- where the number is 9 or ends in 9 replace it with a circle, loop or looped line (similar to nine, looped to the left)

Join these elements up, particularly via the lines and crosses, into a design that looks good to you. Practice will help develop a style.

AN EXAMPLE OF AN EQ SIGIL:

THE MIDNIGHT SUN

'By Thy Name Khep-Ra I invoke Thee, O
Beetle of the Hidden Mastery of Midnight.'
From The Invocation of Horus, March 1904.

THE FIRST PART OF THIS CHAPTER CONCERNS THE RELATIONS
between the Adorations from the Stele of Revealing
and the Tarot in terms of ritual magick. Crowley's verse
translation of the Adorations appears in Chapter III
of The Book of the Law, the first 'verse' – what appears
in chapter one of AL – is a separate matter from these,
insofar as it is not a translation of the hieroglyphics but
a description of the imagery of the stele. It is with the
verse translation that we are concerned here.

Let us consider these Adorations qaballistically,
in terms of the Names of God and magical instructions
both implicit and explicit in their structure and the
context in which they appear in AL itself. Thelemic
scholars agree, on internal evidence, that the third
chapter of AL has two parts, referring to Ra-Hoor-Khuit
and Hoor-Paar-Kraat as twin gods. The subject matter
of the one part is distinct from that of the second;
although they have certain elements in common these
are presented from different angles as it were. The first
part concerns a ritual or rituals, with altar, Cakes of

Light, Stele of Revealing, incense, and etc., the second
with *The Book of the Law* itself, its comment and the
relations of the initiate with the book. The Adorations
introduce the second phase of the chapter, but let us
remind ourselves just how this changeover is made, and
how the Adorations are introduced.

35. The half of the word of Heru-ra-ha, called Hoor-pa-kraat
and Ra- Hoor-Khut.
36. Then said the prophet unto the God:
37. I adore thee in the song –

> I am the Lord of Thebes, and I
> The inspired forth-speaker of Mentu;
> For me unveils the veiled sky
> The self-slain Ankh-af-na-khonsu
> Whose words are truth. I invoke, I greet
> Thy presence, O Ra-Hoor Khuit!

> Unity uttermost showed!
> I adore the might of Thy breath,
> Supreme and terrible God,
> Who makest the gods and death
> To tremble before Thee: –
> I, I adore thee!

> Appear on the throne of Ra!
> Open the ways of the Khu!
> Lighten the ways of the Ka!
> The ways of the Khabs run through
> To stir me or still me!
> Aum! Let it fill me!

38. So that thy light is in me; & its red flame is as a sword in my hand to push thy order. There is a secret door that I shall make to establish thy way in all the quarters, (these are the adorations as thou hast written), as it is said:

> The light is mine; its rays consume
> Me: I have made a secret door
> Into the house of Ra and Tum,
> Of Khephra and of Ahathoor.
> I am thy Theban, O Mentu,
> The prophet Ankh-af-na-khonsu!
>
> By Bes-na-Maut my breast I beat;
> By wise Ta-Nech I weave my spell.
> Show thy star-splendour, O Nuit!
> Bid me within thine House to dwell,
> O winged snake of light, Hadit!
> Abide with me, Ra-Hoor-Khuit!

There are many matters of importance in Thelemic magick which connect with these verses, but let us start with the text itself. Why the sudden interruption of prose after three verses and what exactly is it talking about? Note the odd grammar and apparent shifting of subject 'there is a secret door... into all the quarters, (these are the adorations...)' and then the Adorations, which also speak of a secret door and names four gods connected with the solar quarters.

The literal sense of 'these are the adorations' in context is either that the secret door is the Adorations, or the quarters are the Adorations, or, since a door cannot, or at least should not be referred to as 'these', then either the quarters are the 'these' or the door and the quarters are the 'these'. Since none of these constructions seem to make much sense then, by Crowley's rule (see *The Equinox of the Gods*), a hidden qaballistic meaning may justifiably be suspected.

I HAVE MADE A SECRET DOOR = 253 = Sum of the numbers 1 to 22. What is more, the second, third and fourth lines of the verse following this peculiar interruption of the Adorations each have twenty-two letters. These are the three lines which name the four gods (of the solar quarters) and refer to the secret door mentioned in the prose interruption.

In the Hebrew Kabbalah there is a set of three verses of Genesis, each of 72 letters, which was used to generate 72 three-lettered names, the Shemhamporash or Divided Name which formed the basis of a magical system that was one of the most significant elements of Hebrew Practical Kabbalah, and an enormous influence on the magical traditions derived from it, up to and including the Golden Dawn. If we follow the same procedure with these three lines we obtain a set of twenty-two three lettered Names which may well be every bit as significant in the magick of this Aeon.

1	MIO	12	AED
2	ENF	13	SOO
3	ITK	14	EFF
4	HOH	15	CRA
5	ATE	16	RAH
6	VHP	17	EAA
7	EEH	18	TNT
8	MHR	19	DDH
9	AOA	20	OTO
10	DUA	21	OUO
11	ESN	22	RMR

There are certain very curious factors about this table. Notice that the third through to the ninth Names are all partly formed from the Name of the God Khephra, and the numbers 3, 4, 5 , 6 , 7, 8 and 9 are those associated with the traditional 'seven' planets, Saturn, Jupiter, Mars, Sun, Venus, Mercury, Moon. There are striking resemblances between this schema and the legend of Khephra, which indeed connects closely to central themes of Thelemic magick. Khephra creates seven gods in his creation myth, which combines sophisticated cosmology with sexual magick, see *Gods of the Egyptians* by Wallace Budge for details. (See also the legends of Atum or Tum, which draw on the same themes.)

If we take these twenty two names as being those of Spirits of the Tarot, certain considerations arise. Firstly, there is *Liber 231*, which already gives TWO sets of twenty two names; this dual nature of the occult alphabet is also found in Spare, and in Pete Carroll's interpretation of the 'Alphabet of Desire' we similarly find a dual principle at work. Secondly, the Tarot or *Book of Thoth* involves a particular type of spirit, much as Geomancy does, or even the Yi King. The spirits of the Tarot, despite their varied astrological attributions in various systems are essentially Mercurial spirits, just as the spirits of the geomantic system with all their correspondences are still spirits of Earth, even if some are referred to Mars or to Leo or whatever.

Liber 231 has been the subject of varied kinds of research. Kenneth Grant's *Nightside of Eden* is the best known, however this only deals with the Qliphothic set of names from 231, and involves some very dubious Qabalah besides:

• in terms of gematria (many of the values he gives are irreproducible);

• of letter symbolism (the names in 231 all begin with the English equivalent of the Hebrew letter to which they correspond, yet the numeration of one of the names as given by Grant relies on Ayin to begin the name corresponding to Vau);

• the handling of the correspondences of He and Tzaddi (he switches the attribution of the letters to the cards in accord with Crowley's interpretation of

'Tzaddi is not the Star' but muddles the attributions, for example, the magical power proper to the Star, the power of Astrology, ends up with the Emperor;

Despite its enormous popularity, his interpretation of 231 – with its sensationalism and its extreme solipsist position – has little to recommend it as a Qabalistic system. Having dealt with this let us return to 231 itself.

The two sets of names are distinguished from one another in two main ways. One is called Qliphothic or demonic, the other, as mentioned, refers to Mercurial 'Genii' which as another writer has said, is the plural of Genius. The other distinguishing feature is that the Qliphothic names are all written in English characters and are proper names, while the genii's names include peculiar letter forms reflecting Hebrew and Coptic, and are not proper names at all, but formulaic expressions of several kinds. Some of them include Enochian elements, at least one is a word from Crowley's equally mysterious 'Moon language' and another, which seems at first glance to be wholly composed of letters, proves on closer examination to include 418 in Roman numerals.

The name corresponding to Leo proves to be a thinly disguised version of Crowley's name, using the 'De Kerval' derivation he affected in the *Confessions*, preceded by the Greek letter Theta. While worthy of further investigation by hardy souls there seems to be little of general value in the series. The sigils are another matter entirely, and should prove to be of use in working with the light and dark aspects of the Paths of the Tree of Life. The English gematria values of the Qlippothic names hint at other applications, and may in some cases be read as indicating the forces requiring 'sublimation' at certain particular points of the magicians progress.

The names derived from the adorations from the Stele of Revealing are listed below. These names may be used with the sigils, using the sigils of the 'geniis' for operations of the light and the Qliphothic sigils for operations of the dark. The operator must decide for themselves whether to use the names given by Crowley as well as the English Qaballistic names.

MIO   – MOILOL A of AL/LA /Fool
ENF   – ELNAFI L of LA/AL/Magus
ITK   – ILTIKA W/Saturn/Aquarius/Priestess
HOH   – HOOLHO H/Jupiter/Pisces/Empress
ATE   – ALTIEL S/Mars/Aries/Emperor
VHP   – VOHOPE D/Sun/Leo/Hierophant
EEH   – ELELHO O/Venus/Taurus/Lust
MHR   – MOHORI Z/Mercury/Gemini/Lovers
AOA   – ALOLAL K/Moon/Cancer/Chariot
DUA   – DIULAL V/Moon/Fortuna/Fortuna
ESN   – ELSUNA G/Mercury/Virgo/Hermit
AED   – ALELDI R/Venus/Libra/Justice
SOO   – SUOLOL C/Sun/Fortuna/Hanged Man
EFF   – ELFIFI N/Mars/Scorpio/Death
CRA   – CERIAL Y/Jupiter/Sagittarius/Art
RAH   – RIALHO J/Saturn/Capricorn/Devil
EAA   – ELALAL U/Mars/Fire/Fortress
TNT   – TINATI F/Venus/Air/Star
DDH   – DIDIHO Q/Moon/Earth/Moon
OTO   – OLTIOL B/Sun/Water/Sun
OUO   – OLULOL M/Jupiter/Spirit Active/Aeon
RMR   – RIMORI X/Saturn/Spirit Passive/Universe

I have made some alterations to the Tarot order as used by Crowley and the Golden Dawn; hopefully the reader will have sufficient mental flexibility to cope with these changes. In justification I affirm that no such attribution is written in stone, and the Tarot has undergone many major transformations over the centuries.

These are the names of the twenty two spirits of Mercury whose names and functions are revealed and concealed in *The Book of the Law*. Note the first seven spirits corresponding to the traditional planets, under the rule of Khephra which are to be invoked at Midnight. Note also how Fortuna, Virgo, Libra and Scorpio form a class outside the immediate rule of the Four Sun Gods. Note also that Ahathoor has dominion over eight spirits, which may be invoked at Midday. Two of these (associated with Sagittarius and Capricorn, with their special relationship with the Libra-Scorpio complex) are also under Ra, and may alternatively be invoked at Dawn under His presidency, while the last three spirits are under Tum as well as Ahathoor, and may be invoked at Sunset under His auspices.

The attributions of the last six spirits are complex and mysterious, however the main attribution to the reflected 'Chaldean Order' of the planets is more than sufficient for most purposes. The last four letters of the English Qaballistic Alphabet are not covered by this attribution, they represent the four elements composing 'The Universe', attributed to X.

R	T	K	H	H
A	M	P	A	H
U	E	A	T	O
H	R	A	O	R

The Sigils of Ra, Tum, Khephra and Ahathoor may easily be derived from this magical arrangement of Their Names on the plan of the Tablet of Union from Dee's Enochian system, and the three Names of God which precede the Adorations – Heru-Ra-Ha, Hoor-Pa-Kraat and Ra-Hoor-Khut – can all be found in this arrangement. Sigils of Thoth, Maat and Hathor are also to be found herein, and naturally Hoor and Heru as these Names form parts of the other Names.

The sigil of Khephra is to be used in Rituals of Midnight, when invoking the Genii corresponding to the traditional seven planets. Similarly the sigils of Ra and Tum, and that of Ahathoor are for use when invoking spirits under their presidency at the Solar Stations. The First and Second Keys of Dee's Enochian system are appropriate incantations for working with this system; note that the First Key uses a variant god name in dealing with 'fallen spirits' such as the spirits of the Qliphoth from *Liber 231*.

It will be noted by traditionally minded students that if the seven 'planetary' spirits are to be invoked at Midnight, then some method of planetary days and hours could be implied. Planetary days and hours have a long history, but have no obvious connection with astrological timing or planetary cycles. However, neither do these Genii, they are simply classified under planetary headings for convenience. It is the four quarters of the day that empower them, since in Thelemic magick these times are used to affirm one's identity with the 93 Current, through the adorations from *Liber Resh*. The Genii of Mercury have their place in this schema, since Tahuti is invoked along with Ra-Hoor at each such quarter, and Tahuti may be said to correspond with the Mind of the magician as Ra-Hoor to the Will. It is perhaps these weapons in the magicians armoury, affirmed at these points of the Sun's apparent circuit of the heavens, which give the Genii their power.

The thirty lines of the Adoration in Chapter III are converted into a barbarous invocation (or in traditional terms 'the Supreme Adjuration' or climactic spell) by taking the number of letters in each line and converting them into syllables with the Wakanaba technique:

XU BA MO LAZE TI
WAOL EL QE XU EL
TI MO MO XU EL
WAAL QE UL FI TI
IL GU NA TI XU

and then arranging these syllables into words as follows:

XUBAMO LAZE-TI
WAOL ELQEXUEL,
TIMOMOXUEL,
PETI LAOL XU LAZE,
WAAL QEULFI-TI,
ILGUNATIXU: (N#)

[#N represents the name of the particular Genii invoked.]

When drawing sigils for these spirits the Square of Mercury or the Sun will prove perfectly adequate, however equally 'traditional' geometric Sigils of the Twenty Two Spirits may alternatively be obtained from the grid of sheet 16 with its eighty squares lettered in the 'vertical' order given in the chapter 'The Cipher of AL'.

The manner of doing this is to take the six-lettered name of the spirit and divide it into three two letter syllables. The alphabet is repeated on the grid three times, with two letters over, the first two letters of the name are taken from the first complete alphabet on the left hand side of the grid, so that the sigil begins at the first letter, and a line from it to the position of the second letter completes the first syllable; the next two letters are found in the second complete alphabet, and the third two letter pair in the third alphabet on the right hand side. The exception to this is when the operation is performed at dawn, invoking the spirits under Ra, then the A in the first syllable is taken from the letters left over (AB) in the bottom right hand corner. Tracing a line from the first letter through letters 2 to 6 forms the essential shape of the sigil, which is completed by embellishing the sigil with a circle at the beginning and a wedge or short line at the end of the sigil.

These sigils are called 'The Sigils of AL-Kabala', for the simple reason that if the individual letters of the grid are extended by the rules of Wakanaba then the four letters in the top left hand corner become the 'words' AL-KA/BA-LA. Note that the cipher of II.76 includes the 'word' ABK.

The grid itself may be painted as a 'tablet' with the letters in the appropriate squares. It should not be used until thoroughly consecrated – the preferred method includes placing the tablet on the central altar and on six consecutive days invoking the five elements with the Pentagram ritual given in the section 'Qaballa as Ritual Language'. After this the Tablet can be used in rituals of this system; for example, tracing the appropriate Sigil of AL-Kabala over the Tablet at the climax of the Invocation of Tahuti.

A chant or chants may easily be derived from this grid when extended with Wakanaba techniques. The 80 squares of the grid obviously suggest the words of AL I.46: 'Nothing is a secret key of this law. Sixty-one the Jews call it; I call it eight, eighty, four hundred & eighteen'. Consequently such chants are very appropriate to operations where the void state is desired, or in operations of Tahuti (Eight is the number of Mercury, and this grid concerns both letters and Qaballa, themes particularly attributed to Mercury). An example chant with suggested pronunciation guide is given on the following page.

AL-KABALA CEMODINA ELOLFIPE GUQE HORI
AL-Kabbalah Cairmodeenah Airlolfipay Gukay Hoori

ILSU-JUTI ULELVO-FI WAGUXUHO YO-IL-ZEJU
Eelsu-duty Ulelvo-fee Wahguzoohoh Yoh-eel Zairdue

AL-KABALA CEMODINA OLYO-PEZE QE-AL RIBA
AL-Kabbalah Cairmodeenah Olyo-Pairzay Kay-AL-Reebah

SUCE-TI-DI ULELVO-FI WAGUXUHO
Sookay-Tee-Dee Yule-elvo-fee Wah-goo zoohoh

ILSU-JUTI KAUL-LAVO MOWANAXU OLYO-PEZE QE-AL-RIBA.
Eelsu duty Cahul-Lahvo Mowahnahzoo Olyo-Pairzay Kay AL Reeba.

Such chants are useful when evoking the Mercurial Spirits, and may be combined with the 'Majesty of Godhead' Invocation found in *Liber Israfel* (the original invocation, composed by Allan Bennett, which forms the main text of *Liber Israfel* begins 'O thou Majesty of Godhead' and ends 'Every Spell and Scourge of God may be obedient unto me' – the rest of the text may be omitted and replaced as appropriate to the ritual in hand).

Alternatively, or in addition, a ritual may be composed involving the Adorations from Resh, those from the Stele of Revealing and the Spell derived from it which was given earlier. *Liber LXV* begins with a splendid invocation of use in Midnight operations, while Chapter V (attributed to Mercury) of *Liber VII* could also be appropriately employed with this system, and there is a splendid rhymed invocation of Thoth in the Opening of *Liber Pyramidos*. As said above, the First and Second Keys of Dee's Enochian schema also have their place among these Rituals of Midnight.

A major ritual, even so far as evocation to visible appearance, may readily be developed from these materials as the vehicle of effective technique. Such operations are certainly sophisticated and arduous, but comparison with the Golden Dawn methods (see the Invocation of Tapthartharath in Crowley's *Equinox* I.3.) has consistently shown them to be both less time consuming and more effective.

THE SIXFOLD CROSS

SINCE WE HAVE DECIDED TO DEAL WITH SOME OF THE MAGICAL connections of Christianity in this book it may be as well to remark upon a curiosity of old style Qabalism, with its predilection for geometry and geometrical solids in particular. In the Golden Dawn ritual of the 32nd path the candidate is presented with a 'Greek Cubical Cross'. It is equal-armed and composed of four cubes surrounding a fifth. When arranged in this fashion eight of the total of thirty sides are concealed, leaving twenty two exposed. These were attributed to the letters of the Hebrew alphabet. The 32nd Path is attributed to the Tarot Trump 'The Universe', the literal meaning of the Hebrew letter attributed to it is 'a cross', and it is the 22nd letter. The cross represents the elements in balance (the four arms and spirit in the centre, and the three 'Elemental' Mother Letters are emblazoned across it. As a synthetic symbol it is very pleasing and appropriate, and much could come of a meditation upon its formation.

Similar items appear throughout the initiations, as tokens enabling the Candidate to enter the region concerned. Upon finally attaining to Adeptus Minor – the whole focus of the system, and with its associations with the Holy Guardian Angel the focus of Crowley's 'mission to mankind' – the initiate receives a similar item, on a much grander scale. This is the Rose Cross Lamen, formed of six squares, a true crucifix or Calvary

Cross, thus associating the sacrificial formula of Christianity with the complex of ideas corresponding to the sixth sephira, Tiphereth. Upon its centre is a Rose of 22 petals, with the Hebrew alphabet arranged in three whorls. The upper square is attributed to air, the right to water and the left to fire. The square below the Rose is attributed to Spirit, whilst the lowest square corresponds to earth.

Crowley used a similar item, a Cross of six squares set with a topaz in the centre, the whole made of wood and painted vermilion, as a portable skrying tool in his exploration of the Thirty Aethyrs (see *The Vision and the Voice*). Such devices, combining geometrical and qaballistic symbolism, have a distinguished place in the Mystery Schools. The harmonising of the two schemes makes them complex representations of the Universe. The geometrical building blocks of creation, and the Holy letters, represented the ideas behind these forms.

These Gnostic cosmological models mirror archetypal structures implicit in the Microcosmic and Macrocosmic worlds. No Western school of any degree of importance lacks such a model – those described above are 'Christian Cabbalism' – yet neither Achad nor Crowley advanced far down the path of supplying or discovering such three dimensional models. The reasons for this extend into uncharted territory, but at base both were too deeply attuned to the partially destroyed Hebrew/G.·.D.·. model to extrapolate along original lines with *The Book of the Law* itself.

However, for those of the English Qaballistic school there are no such contradictions. The occult investigation of the Qaballa of *AL* has to be performed with discipline and detachment. It is imperative above all that the investigator does not impose preconceived notions onto the numerical structures, but allows them to speak for themselves. In this way the current informing *AL* supplies 'New Symbols'.

Enough introduction: the model I wish to describe now combines the qualities of the two former, but is a radical departure from both. The Sixfold Cross has many properties of qaballistic and geometrical significance. Firstly the number of cubes of which it is composed suggests Tiphereth, the sixth Sephira; its cruciform shape suggests the inner Gnostic sense of the Christ figure.

The number of junctions between cubes is five, suggesting Spirit balancing and informing the four elements, traditionally symbolised by turning the fourfold Tetragrammaton into the fivefold name of Jesus by the addition of the letter of Spirit, also representing the Rosicrucian secret of the Sun-Venus cycle. This cycle is a double cycle. While five Inferior Conjunctions are formed over eight years, a concurrent sequence of Superior Conjunctions is also producing a Pentagram. The number of concealed faces of our Cross is of course ten, representing both this double cycle and the Sephirothic archetypes. These are concealed behind the more complex and material ideas of the twenty six revealed faces representing our alphabet.

Taking the ten 'Hidden Faces' to represent the English ideas associated by gematria with the Sephirothic numbers is an important element in understanding this complex symbol. The meanings of the Hidden Faces in the vertical component of the Sixfold Cross reveal a great deal about the structure of the Sun-Venus ritual, while the meanings in the horizontal component refer to the combined forces at work in the ritual. This is best left to the ingeniuum of the magician to work out.

Correspondences fanatics constantly attempt to attribute the Outer Planets to the letters. The initiate on the other hand sees that the Sephiroth and in particular the Supernals, even in their 'mundane chakra' or planetary mode, simply do not operate on the same level as the more complex and materialised ideas represented by the Paths/Letters. We should carefully distinguish the Path attributed to a planetary idea from the Sphere bearing a similar planetary correspondence.

The attribution of the alphabet used in English Qaballa (first published in *The Equinox: British Journal of Thelema*, Volume One, No. 1) distinguishes very precisely by dealing with the planets through the medium of their zodiacal houses. The Transpersonal planets likewise do not operate on the same level as the Seven 'inner' or personal planets; the sevenfold and threefold Sephirothic complexes are quite distinct. As Pluto will have traversed the entire zodiac 'under human observation' by the year 2184, assuming civilisation and the radio telescope last that long, an attribution of the Outer Planets to the Letters may then become possible.

The elemental and planetary schemes are often perceived as watertight categories, whereas in the zodiac, and in the paths of the Tree they are in fact intermixed. There are thus planetary associations to the so-called elemental grades. The diagrams and attributions in so many occult books appear to be static, departmental structures, despite the regular use of such words as 'the Path', 'Going' and so forth in relation to them.

Astrology, as a changing, combining and recombining, multifaceted and essentially feminine structure concurrent with our sensory experience in time, is the physical manifestation of the mobile reality represented imperfectly by those seemingly static figures. Once this is taken on board traditional Qabalistic ideas become far more lucid. For, while the astrological techniques enable one to deal with ongoing events and experiences, it is through the 'mobilised' Qaballa with its extensive permutations and nuances that we are able to see beyond these levels of reality to their less manifest analogues. In this way the two complement each other perfectly. They are not separate systems, but twin pillars of the Temple of Wisdom.

The allocation of the letters to the Sixfold Cross is extremely straightforward, and demonstrates the perfection implicit in the correspondences of the letters (there are analogies also with the G∴D∴ Badge of the 32nd Path and the 5=6 Rose Cross Lamen). Briefly, there are fourteen faces surrounding the Cross, corresponding to the reflected sevenfold scheme in the alphabetic correspondences. Accordingly, the first seven planetary letters are allocated to the topmost square and the six subsequent squares going clockwise. In this way the letter representing the Priestess, (the Path reaching to the highest comprehension of Kether) is at the top of the Cross, She is also Isis or Nuit, the Starry Heaven marking the physical limits of human comprehension. Then the second planetary septenary of letters is attributed to the lowest square and the six subsequent squares in a clockwise direction. In this way, alarming as it may seem, the face corresponding

to the Tarot 'Devil' is at the base of the Cross, a new
light on traditional 'infernal' inverted crosses. Further
significant details emerge when both series are in place.
For example, at one end of the horizontal bar of the
Cross is a Solar letter, and at the other one of Venus. In
this way the attributions extend the links between the
ideas discussed above when dealing with the physical
structure of the figure.

There are twelve letters remaining of which ten are
attributed to a reflected sequence of the five elements.
Following the precedent of the Rose Cross Lamen these
are attributed as Air above centre, Fire left and Water
right of centre, Spirit directly below centre and Earth at
the base of the elongated arm. This applies to the series
of elemental letters on the two faces of the Cross. In the
central square of the two elemental crosses go the letters
A and L on the face of the Cross appropriate to each.
This central point is in fact the 'Beginning' rather than
the end and represents the interaction of None and Two
in Thelemic cosmology.

Another point of direct relevance here is the
EQ analysis of JESUS CHRIST. Whereas formerly
'Christian Cabbalism' saw Jesus as harmonising the
Fourfold Elemental Kingdom of the Creator (in the
same way Tiphereth crowns the 'Elemental Grades'),
the EQ analysis extends this, for by 'counting well'
JESUS with CHRIST we obtain 813, the value of the
combined planetary gematrias from Pluto = 76 through
to Moon = 49. This is wholly in accord with Gnostico-
Hermetic ideas of Christ as the guide through the Seven
planetary veils to the Supernals above. The connection
between Jesus and Set is implicit in this analysis also, for

the number of letters in the planetary titles, from Pluto to the Moon is 54, the value of the Name SET.

In Hebrew Kabbalah the Name YHVH is pre-eminent, and Kabbalistic techniques involving it are central to many areas of Practical Kabbalah. One important theme involves the Permutations of the letters of this Name. The Name YHVH can be permutated 54 different ways, a feature it shares with the Thelemic Tetragrammaton: HOOR. The Name itself has four letters, and in EQ FOUR = 54. Since each permutation of the Name also consists of four letters, the total number of letters is 216, which is the number of letters in the Shemhamporash (72 three lettered names = 216), but also the value in EQ of RA+TUM+KHEPHRA+AHATHOOR.

INCANTATION

'grammarians... will change their concepts.
Arithmeticians will develop a new notion of
number... geometers will find the principles
of their art insufficiently established... After
studying the treatise, the cabalists will recognize
that their art is universal and not, as had been
thought, confined to the hebrew language;
this new cabala, exemplified by the Monas
Hieroglyphica, will reveal the secrets of the
entire creation through new arts and methods.'
John Dee, *The Hieroglyphic Monad.*

ARTIFICIAL AND MAGICAL LANGUAGES ARE A PART OF
qaballistic magick with an enduring fascination. Dee's
Enochian system was intended to supersede Hebrew;
attempts to relink the two are retrogressive and miss
Dee's real purpose, which was way ahead of his time.
'Thus you see here, the Necessity of this Tongue: The
Excellency of it, And the Cause why it is preferred
before that which you call Hebrew: For it is written
Every lesser consenteth to his greater. I trust this is
sufficient.' The mysterious 'it is written' can only mean
that the 'less' (the inferior Hebrew) 'consenteth' (agrees
with, i.e. the useful elements of the Hebrew system will
not be lost by being superseded by the Enochian, but
transcended) 'to his greater' (the Enochian system, the

'real' language of the Angels, as opposed to 'that which you call Hebrew' which is held by both Dee and his angels to have degenerated from its pristine original). Contrary to orthodox Golden Dawn opinion the Enochian language is, in the words of David Allen Hulse: 'an artificial magical language, but such a premise does not diminish its magical efficacy one iota.'

Barbarous names in traditional magick were frequently obtained by means of the technique of permutation, which may be studied in Agrippa and in Kaplan's *Meditation and Kabbalah*. A great practical advantage of the permutation method was that names and words could be devised as necessary rather than slavishly copied from older sources. Agrippa emphasises that these and similar techniques may be used with Latin, Greek and other alphabets as well as Hebrew.

The Counting Well technique provides a ready means of permutation without the theological or linguistic problems involved in the older systems. It does so not by means of an 'anglified' rendition of the Hebrew system, but by developing upon a technique at the heart of the EQ system itself. Each square (or more properly, grid) obtained by counting well is essentially a series of numerical permutations of the original 'Double Word'. All that needs to be done is to turn these numerical permutations back into letters and syllables.

In order to do this we first look at the numbers in the scale 1 to 26, since these are already attributed to the English Alphabet. However, counting well gives numbers in the range 2 to 52. Numbers above 26 are expressed in terms of their digits, i.e. 27 as 2 and 7. Simply turning each number into its letter equivalent will produce words superficially resembling both Dee's and Bertiaux's artificial languages. The problem then is how to pronounce them. Hebrew manages this either through a method of attributing vowel points to such artificial words (some of which then become actual Hebrew words) or taking D as Da on the basis that D's name is *dAleth*.

This identical method was later borrowed by the Golden Dawn to render Enochian pronounceable, a not altogether satisfactory grafting from one system to another. The system from which this was 'borrowed' involves the famous 'Shemhamphorash', the 'Divided' or 'Seventy-two fold' Name. This played a major part in Hebrew Practical Kabbalah in the system of Abraham Abulafia (1240 to 1300). This book is hardly the place for an extended discussion of this great Pre-Zohar Kabbalist (see Scholem's *Major Trends in Jewish Mysticism* and Kaplan's *Meditation and Kabbalah*), but it is worth emphasising that, while the Golden Dawn's Qabalah has been shown to owe much to Isaac Luria, the system of Abulafia has far more to offer the modern 'Practical Qaballist'. In the following quotation Kaplan seems to be referring to the 'Proto-language' concept we encountered earlier:

'Take in your hand a scribe's pen. Write speedily, letting your tongue utter the words with a pleasant melody, very slowly. Understand the words that leave your lips. The words can consist of anything that you desire, in any language that you desire, for you must return all languages to their original substance. I have alluded to this elsewhere... but this is its proper place...' From Aryeh Kaplan's *Meditation and Kabbalah*.

English Qaballa has had many inspired moments in the course of its development and the solution to the problem of pronunciation described above is yet another example of 'the hand of the inscrutable gods' in it all. The vowels in the EQ alphabet series are in the order AOUIE, they have the combined value of 73 = MANTRA, POWER, RUNES, GIANT. Among the consonants the letter L has a special place as an element of AL and LA. Its shape also suggests the horizontal and vertical components of a graph or grid. In order to render the other consonants pronounceable they require one or other of these vowels, while a good case can be made for pairing the vowels with the letter L, and for making L into LA as reflex of AL.

A square showing which vowel corresponds with which consonants is shown below. The order of the vowels and consonants is unchanged, they have simply been separated in order to place them in the square. The letter L is the factor which balances them, as appropriate to its attribution to Libra in 'Old Letters'.

A | W K N B
O | H V Y M
I | S G J X
E | Z C Q P

The first line gives us WA KA NA BA, for which reason this technique is called Wakanaba or Wakan. The complete alphabet then can be expressed as:

AL LA WA HO SU DI OL ZE KA VO GU RI CE

NA YO JU UL FI QE BA MO XE IL TI EL PE

This can be turned into a chanted spell, the eight pairs of 'triplets' balanced rhythmically against each other and the two last syllables breaking the rhythm as an exclamation. The rhythmic section aids the passive contemplation of an image, sigil or square; the breaking of the rhythm with exclamation actively internalises or charges the symbol.

ALLAWA, HOSUDI;
OLZEKA,VOGURI;
CENAYO, JUULFI;
QEBAMO, XUILTI:
EL PE!

For convenience the numbers 27 to 52 are listed in Wakan form here, but with a little experiment and familiarisation the student will no longer find it necessary to consult these tables.

27	LA-OL	40	HO-OL
28	LA-ZE	41	HO-AL
29	LA-KA	42	HO-LA
30	WA-OL	43	HO-WA
31	WA-AL	44	HO-HO
32	WA-LA	45	HO-SU
33	WA-WA	46	HO-DI
34	WA-HO	47	HO-OL
35	WA-SU	48	HO-ZE
36	WA-DI	49	HO-KA
37	WA-OL	50	HO-OL
38	WA-ZE	51	HO-AL
39	WA-KA	52	HO-LA

With this pronunciation aid we can now turn to the numbers in our squares. 27 now becomes LA-OL, 43 becomes HO-WA and so on. Any number can be expressed, and more importantly the words of power so derived are all pronounceable, however alien they may sound. The large number of vowels in each 'spell' give an ecstatic edge to the chants which is partly why the Gnostics (and even church choirs) made such great use of them.

Our Square of Babalon can now be turned into a Spell of Babalon as follows:

HO-OL, MO, HO-OL, MO, XU, LA-OL, WA-HO,
MO, LA, MO, LA, WA, ZE, YO,
HO-OL, MO, HO-OL, MO, XU, LA-OL, WA-HO,
MO, LA, MO, LA, WA, ZE, YO,
XU, WA, XU, WA, HO,KA, JU,
LA-OL, ZE, LA-OL, ZE, KA, NA, MO,
WA-HO, YO, WA-HO, YO, JU, MO, LA-ZE,

A good habit for pronouncing the vowel sounds is A = Ah, O = Oh, U = Oo, I = Eee, E = Eh/Airh. This will be found to produce sonorous and magically/mantrically effective sounds (this applies fairly well as a rule of thumb in the use of old Gnostic god-names etc.; only armchair wizards would pronounce IAO as Eye Aye Oh rather than Eeaaoh).

RESULTS MAGICK WITH WAKANABA

A purely 'results-magick' application of the Wakanaba technique is in 'mantric-sigils', when the original stated purpose is disguised not by rearrangement of syllables of the original sentence, but by reducing each word in the statement to its gematria value and converting those values into sounds by means of the Wakanaba technique. To take a classic example from Austin Spare, the intention:

'This my will to have the strength of a tiger'

gives us the gematria values: 56 36 30 31 40 53 119 25 1 95

converting these by means of the Wakanaba technique we obtain:

SUDI WADI WAOL WALA HOOL SUWA ALALKA LASU AL KASU

which may be converted into phrases according to taste, for example:

SUDIWADI WAOLWA, OLWALA HOOL: SUWA ALALKA, LASU ALKASU!

Alternatively (or in addition) we can total the entire statement of intent:

56+36+30+31+40+53+119+25+1+95=486

and convert 486 via Wakanaba, obtaining the word SUZEDI, which can be used as a mantric word in its own right or added to the above as the climactic word of a chanted spell. The methods of potentising such spells are fairly numerous and are to be found in many contemporary works on chaos magick, sexual occultism and sigil techniques. The first and foremost is simply to repeat the mantra while seated in asana, over and over again thus inducing an altered state of consciousness and forgetfulness of the magical intention. A species of glossolalia will frequently result if the mantra is repeated out loud, and while this should not be forced or over-indulged, neither should it be inhibited or suppressed.

Other means of producing incantations and mantras from Magick Squares (including the column totals and combined values) may readily be evolved:

A) the Wakan method, where 128 equals ALLAZE

B) the gematria method, finding or constructing a Name with the value 128, such as BAPHOMET or BES-NA-MAUT.

C) The number spelt 'in full', ONE TWO EIGHT gives 46, 34 and 87, giving us the Names: I-I, ABRA, FALUTLI. (Or since 12 substitutes for 1 in the A.M.E.N. schema take 89 in place of 46 and use a Name of that value, thus NU-HAD-IT, ABRA, FALUTLI).

D) a combination of these, for example: AL (Wakan), ABRA (gematria of number spelt), ZE (Wakan), thus AL-ABRA-ZE.

Further methods are readily devised with some experience and intuition.

The Fifty Gates & Sri Yantra

EQ PROVIDES ADDITIONAL METHODS OF INTERPRETING the numbers in these grids for magical use. As I said earlier the grids will provide values in the range 2 to 52. *The Book of the Law,* together with the other Class A writings, provides a wealth of names and sounds (the spell in the 'Moon Language' for example) which can be used in Practical Qaballa. Of these a great many fall in the range 2 to 52 and the few deficiencies are readily supplied by combining vowels and consonants. In this way a selection of sounds with an value equal to the range of grid squares encountered can be used to turn any square into a chant with the same numerical value as the square (both in detail and in total). As said earlier, the permutation method is traditionally held to be a means of ingress into the initiatory process called the Fifty Gates.

There are several contexts in qaballistic literature where 70 and 50 represent 72 and 52 rounded down. There are excellent reasons for supposing that the 51 or 52 categories of this system should be understood as essentially equivalent to the Fifty Gates of the Hebrew system and its possible ancestor or relative, the Sri Yantra – the excess of 1 or 2 digits should be explained as poetic license rather than Kabbalistic inaccuracy. The traditional Hebrew scheme could with some justice be said to consist of 49 gates, since not even Moses ever entered the 50th! Research shows that the Fifty Gates derives from 'pre-10 commandments' rites of the Hebrews, extended over seven weeks (49 days) with a climactic day of communion. That this ancient practice connects with the origins of the Sri Yantra is a not unreasonable supposition. A yantra containing a 7x7 grid (the Venus square) is known, and is as ancient as the Sri Yantra itself.

One formulation of the Hebrew system of Fifty Gates involves the projection of the ten Sephiroth into Seven Palaces (Malkuth and Yesod in the lowest palace, the Supernal Triad in the highest palace and the remaining Sephiroth one per palace), each containing seven gates (as each palace itself contains its own tree in seven palaces). The number 49 is particularly connected with Venus (7 x 7) whose symbol contains the entire Tree of Life, and with the Moon (MOON = 49). The system proposed here has 51 categories, or 17 by 3. This too connects with Venus, both through the number symbols of 1 and 7 (1 = ONE = 46 = WOMAN, and 7 is the number of Venus) and because 17 (XVII) corresponds to The Star in the Tarot (Oswald Wirth connects this trump with Sun-Venus conjunctions, also the eight pointed star is the Sumerian symbol for Venus, on account of her eight year cycle through her phases and of her fivefold conjunctions with the Sun).

A table listing many of the 'barbarous name' equivalents of the series 2 to 52 follows:

2	A-A.	19	ASAR. AF. LU.	36	AIWAZ. AMN. OHE. IOD.
3	AL. LA. A-A-A.	20	WA-YA.	37	NI.
4	WA.	21	AB.	38	AIWASS. NIA. MU.YAMA.
5	AH. HA.	22	SU.	39	AUM. REL.
6	SA.	23	I. AMA.	40	CHI.
7	O.	24	LAM.	41	PAN. HADES. UT. TU.
8	OA.	25	TA.	42	QADOSH.
9	ZA.	26	KU.	43	NOX. OURDA.
10	AH-AH. KA.	27	PA. EL. LE. WI.	44	AUM-HA.
11	HAD. HO. OH.	28	ANKH. GU.	45	HORUS. PA-SA-GA. HUT.
12	GA.	29	ASI.	46	I-I.
13	RA.	30	HOOR. CHAOS. IO. KHU. SE.	47	MAAT. TI. KRAAT. AMN-HO.
14	O-O.	31	NU. IAO. OAI.	48	ASAR-ISA. MALAI.
15	NA. AN.	32	KAABA. TAO.	49	MARY. EROS. BALAE.
16	YA. OAZ.	33	IOAI.	50	BES. COPH. KUT.
17	U.	34	AL. OAI. ABRA.	51	KRAATH. PE. U-U-U. LATAI.
18	AU.	35	FU.	52	ADONAI. MOAI. HATHOR.

This may be extended by taking the five vowels and enumerating their combinations:

AA=2	OA=8	UA=18	IA=24	EA=26
AO=8	OO=14	UO=24	IO=30	EO=32
AU=18	OU=24	UU=34	IU=40	EU=42
AI=24	OI=30	UI=40	II=46	EI=48
AE=26	OE=32	UE=42	IE=48	EE=50

The student can of course devise other combinations of three or more vowels, and English or other words of the appropriate value can have their letters transposed to produce barbarous names. For example, the words with value 32 in the table above could become ABAKA and AOT (which latter word appears in the climax of the Bornless Rite). Note that the numerical range of the vowel combinations above is 2 to 50, a 49-fold classification.

By means of this table we may compose another Babalon spell:

CHI AB WA AB SU PA O
AB A-A AB A-A AL OA NA
CHI AB WA AB SU PA O
AB A-A AB A-A AL OA NA
SU AL SU AL WA ZA OAZ
PA OA PA OA AZ O-O AB
AL-OAI NA ABRA NA OAZ BA ANKH

Take note that the 52-fold table culminates with
ADONAI, representing the Holy Guardian Angel
as guide across the Abyss, and with HATHOR, the
Egyptian goddess of Love and Venus, a form of Isis
reminiscent of Babalon. This is the highest of the Gates
and the culmination of the initiatory experience. It is
to be noted that Adonai is often portrayed as a Goddess
and has links with the Trump the High Priestess. The
Egyptian Venus, Hathor, is a fitting correspondence for
the mystical marriage of adept and angel. Her name
means 'House of Horus' ('the name of thy house'),
similarly Babalon means 'Gate of (the God) On'.
This is a very significant association – it detaches the
traditional Hebrew methodology from the Judaeo-
Christian religious model and links it firmly to the
Thelemic cosmogony as delineated in the Class A and
the *Vision and the Voice*.

A fascinating connection between this system and
the Tantras emerges when we consider the foremost
tantric symbol of the Goddess is the Sri Yantra which
has 51 divisions corresponding to the letters of the
Sanskrit alphabet (do not be confused to find different
sources mentioning 50, 51 and 52 letters). While there
is no exact match between the Hebrew and Indian
systems, the parallels are extensive. The Sri Yantra is
undoubtedly the older of the two systems, and the likely
source of the Hebrew schema.

Of course both Hebrew and Sanskrit are ritual
languages adapted to particular cultures and forms
of religious expression, while the English Qaballa is
a ritual language appropriate to our own. It is curious
indeed that no correlation between the 50 Gates and

the Sri Yantra seems to have been suspected by students
of the older systems. It was discovered solely through
work with the English Qaballa.

The association with the Sri Yantra is significant
for a variety of interconnected reasons. The Sanskrit
language is the primal ancestor of English, and Tantric
usage of the Sanskrit Alphabet connects strongly with
the mantric/qaballistic theme we are considering.
The entire alphabet is associated with the Goddess
in the Tantric system, She is 'made of mantra', and
the correspondences of the 51 divisions of the yantra
point to the essentially 'Astro-qaballistic' nature of
this conception. She is in many ways synonymous with
the Thelemic Goddesses, sharing many attributes with
them. These include the connection with Time as an
astrological phenomenon, the description of 'Scarlet
Woman', the sexual nature of Her worship, and so on.
There are too many sources in Thelemic and western
Tantric studies which support this connection for me to
need to labour the point.

This matching of the old system of the Fifty Gates
with Thelemic magick is inherent in the numerical
structure of English as a Holy Tongue. Crowley's
Vision and the Voice used Enochian instead of Hebrew
for magical purposes. Despite this use of a language
other than Hebrew a curious effect may be noticed
throughout the course of *The Vision and the Voice* where
older Qabalistic concepts are revitalised in a new
Thelemic form. EQ not only matches the Fifty Gates
and similar Hebraic systems, but also incorporates the
'improvements' Crowley discovered in his exploration
of the Aethyrs. Where *The Vision and the Voice* (and

Thelemic magick as derived from the Golden Dawn) achieves this by mingling systems – with occasional mismatches – pure numerical necessity more often than not produces results with EQ that harmonise these themes into a unified schema.

An obvious example of this is in the word NOX, which is termed 'The Key of the Abyss' in *The Vision and the Voice*, and appears in the Class A literature with the same sense. The 'Babe of the Abyss' in Crowley's system is the culmination of the work in Chesed (Exempt Adept). If we arrange our numerical series 2 to 52 in seven palaces, each containing seven numbers or names (disregarding for now the two left over) then the last number in the palace of Chesed is 43 = NOX. This can only represent 'the Voluntary Emancipation of the Exempt Adept from his Adeptship'. Moreover the Sri Yantra's triangular 'petals' are 43 in number, the Square and Cross motif which surrounds it supplying the additional eight divisions.

These parallels are frequent, produced only by mathematical necessity, and reveal an underlying structure to language and consciousness. Both the Fifty Gates and the Sri Yantra are used in two main ways, the involutionary and the evolutionary. More simply, one may work from the bottom to the top and vice versa with the Hebrew schema and from the centre out and vice versa with the Sanskrit schema. In both systems we see a formulation of a universe from the simple to the complex in graduated stages, in both cases there is a system of correspondences involving celestial and astrological hierarchies, in both cases there is a correlation between the levels of the schema and the human anatomy/chakra system. The parallels could not be more exact, but intriguing though they are we should appreciate the lesson that this 'discovery' came about through work with a 'living' Holy Tongue.

Persistent use of mantras and spells will access many levels of consciousness as well as provide magical results appropriate to the talismans constructed by these methods. This is a reminder of Crowley's oft repeated dictum that each operation of magick should be a necessary step on the path of initiation, that no 'results magick' should be undertaken other than to facilitate the Great Work. The adept who uses these squares will be accessing powers and potencies of incalculable power, and while they will assist the adept in the Great Work they will not assist when the operation is undertaken lightly or for purposes opposed to the supreme goal of the individual concerned. For the false adept the result may be nothing at all on the one hand, or madness and death on the other.

An appropriate ritual format for use with the Fifty Gates is to be found in the verse translation of the reverse of the Stele of Revealing. These inscriptions are taken from the Egyptian *Book of the Dead* and relate to the passage through the Judgement Hall of the 42 Assessors. An example of the adaptation of this ritual for the ascent of the Middle Pillar from the Sphere of the Elements through Luna and on to the Sphere of the Sun follows here.

A.M.E.N. RITUAL FROM THE STELE

Perform the Invoking Ritual of the Pentagram with Enochian Sigils.
Then trace the invoking Pentagram of Earth in the four quarters
with the Names:
ISIS-HATHOR, MAUT, AOUIE, FIAT.

Facing West with hand on heart say:

My Heart, My Mother, My Heart, My Mother
My Heart which I had upon Earth
Do not witness against Me before the Lord of the West
Since I have united the Earth and Sky with the West
While I lived upon Earth.

Then trace the invoking Hexagram of the Moon in the four quarters
with the Names:
QADOSH-ISIS, IACCHUS, SHOSINEL, MARY.

Face West again and raising the hand in the Sign of Mentu say:

O Upraised Arm of the Shining Moon
May I go forth among the multitudes
And pass through the doors and dwell
Among Ye in the Region of Stars
That I may go forth as I please
Among those living on Earth.

Now trace the Invoking Hexagram of the Beast in the four quarters
with the Names:
JESUS, BES, ISIS, AIWAZ.

Hail Thou that art exalted, hail Thou that art adored
The Great One of Power, the Divine Soul feared by the gods,
Thou who blazest upon Thy Mighty Throne, make a path
For My Soul, My Spirit, My Shadow that I may shine
Forth as a Divine Living One in the Place of Ra, Tum, Khephra,
Hathor

It is interesting to note that the Hebrew Kabbalists' so-called 42 lettered name of God is attributed to the schema of the seven palaces, six letters per palace – note the 42-fold table of the Enochian system, too. The ritual Pyramidos is also a good resource for ritual work in this area. Similarly, tantric usage of the Sri Yantra can be readily adapted for use with English mantras, an event predicted in the tantras themselves: 'There will be born at London English folk whose mantra for worship is in the Phiranga (English) language, who will be undefeated in battle and Lords of the World.' *Merutantra*, XXIII Prakasha (17th century). The basic principle is one of magical catharsis during a ritual ascent of the cosmic ladder, in the process confronting the 'planetary devils', and by the process of transforming them into 'angels' or agencies of will, the corresponding chakra of the magician is opened and s/he receives an interior initiation. A species of transcendental morality is often connected with this schema, but conventional morality is not sufficient. Bear in mind that in etymology the word *virtue* has the same root as the word *virile*.

QABALLISTIC MEDITATION

QABALLISTIC MEDITATION IS AN IMPORTANT ASPECT OF this system, and many assumptions are based on its results, making much incomprehensible without personal experience. The bare bones are not dissimilar to the Middle Pillar exercise of Israel Regardie, but the similarity is to some extent superficial, as will emerge in the course of this section. The Middle Pillar Exercise, for those who are unacquainted with it, is a series of practical instructions expanded from the papers of the Golden Dawn.

The Exercise has much in common with certain tantric practices, indeed Regardie draws attention to a work titled *The Secret of the Golden Flower* which shows this relationship quite clearly. The shortcomings of the technique as it stands are a) its brevity, b) its variants, some of which are far less germane to our purpose than others, though useful in other spheres (the method performed standing up is useful in the context of the Pentagram Ritual, for instance) and c) its lack of the true automatic quality necessary to breach the gates of the Astral Plane. The strength of the technique lies in its compatibility with the Pentagram, Vibration of God-Names et al, and its sound qaballistic structure. Those who are familiar with the Middle Pillar Exercise and with the pranayama exercises of Crowley's *Liber E* will readily assimilate the ideas I am about to outline. In order to facilitate the integration of these ideas and the technique into the framework of this work, and to enable the student unfamiliar with the method to understand what is to follow, I will first discuss some details.

1. Before undertaking this work, it is essential that the operator is already familiar with the English Qaballa and with *AL*, and perhaps the other Class A writings. Besides this, a degree of preparation with ritual exercises is called for, so that the Pentagram ritual will be performed daily, twice at the least. The effect of this is to balance and integrate the 'Elemental' forces in the magician's make-up. As well as this, it is a good idea to become extremely familiar with the Bornless Rite. This is especially the case if the meditation is to form part of a Magical Retirement as described under heading no. 7 below. In this case, the operator will perform the Bornless Ritual daily: at dawn, noon, sundown and midnight, in his physical body at first, later in the mental body, and as proficiency in the technique described is attained, in the astral body.

2. *Liber E* contains, among other things, a programme of pranayama exercises similar in most respects to the standard yogic techniques, with one essential distinction. This new element is an example of Crowley's genius, and cannot be understood except by reference to various passages of his records and other snippets which were never properly systematised, or by thorough understanding of the automation of the physical processes in yoga and kindred methods, not generally known in the

West. Essentially, the difference consists of the use of a watch to measure the breath cycles, rather than the traditional use of counting heartbeats or simply counting off seconds. The problem with these latter methods is that the heart and mind are subject to fluctuation, so that the rhythm of breath is in fact subject to irregularities beyond the practitioner's ability to control or even detect. The use of a watch removes this imperfection and truly automates the process, with the result that the exercises are very much more effective in terms of time and effort. Unfortunately, the cycles Crowley advocates are far too strenuous to allow for the other essential feature of this technique, which is utter relaxation.

3. The relaxation methods described in Regardie's book *The Middle Pillar* are excellent, and should be used. Briefly they consist of laying down and tensing the whole body. This tension is then relaxed, the idea being that you cannot tell how unrelaxed you are until you consciously tense up and relax. This principle is applied in detail so that, for instance, starting with the toes, one tenses and relaxes them, then the feet, then the ankles, lower legs, thighs and so forth. The difference here between Regardie's method and this is that due to the presence of a watch the practitioner must have their head supported by pillows, so that the relaxing of the neck becomes more critical than might otherwise be the case. Since many Westerners have problems with the throat chakra regardless of the nature of the techniques in use there is a good case to be made for 'ritualising' this problem in this manner anyway.

4. The meditation proper begins with the visualisation of a sphere of white brilliance above the head. Once this is achieved, the practitioner commences to vibrate the Divine Names appropriate to the sphere. This is accompanied with the cultivation of feelings of love and reverence towards the sphere, which represents Kether in the Hebrew schema.

5. The practitioner goes on to add the other spheres of the Middle Pillar, including Da'ath, all in white light, all with their appropriate Divine Names absorbed and vibrated with the breath cycle.

6. The breath cycle itself should be simple, and consists of four parts: exhalation, holding out, inhalation, holding in. The rhythm to a large extent depends on the psychic constitution of the operator. As a general rule, this may be worked out astrologically – Earth and Water signs using a cycle based on two and its multiples, Fire and Air signs a cycle based on three and its multiples. E.g.: Earth and Water 4 out, 2 hold, 4 in, 2 hold (this may be intensified as the operator gains proficiency to 8 out, 4 hold, 8 in, 4 hold). In the case of Fire and Air signs this will be 6-3-6-3 and 9-6-9-6. This rule may not hold universally, but the nature of the cycle best suited to the individual may be worked out by a close examination of the natal chart, weighing active and passive factors to obtain the required picture.

7. The various methods of circulating light described in Regardie's book may be employed if desired; however, the student may well find that things take their own course along similar lines. The important thing is to seek to extend the period of practice as far as possible. It should be done daily, at the same time, and the student should realise that one hour is scarcely sufficient. What is sufficient? This is imponderable, but as a general rule the student should be aiming at a period of three hours per session. Obviously this makes for great difficulties in day-to-day life, so that simpler and less extended versions of the exercise are desirable. However, at some point in your career as a magician, and the sooner the better, for reasons of health, vitality and enthusiasm, you should undertake a 'Magical Retirement' with this technique as the basis, along the lines of the Abramelin operation. While a certain degree of emotional and mental maturity is desirable with this methodology, it is also essential that the student's health and vigour be at its peak, so that preferably the operator will be between 25 and 45 years of age.

8. The method of concentration employed in this technique is controlled association. By this is meant that the student will restrict their thoughts to the correspondences, symbolic and numerical, to the Sphere on which they are working. Thus when 'Kether' is being cultivated, the range of thoughts will be restricted to its symbols, and to the words and phrases which are numerically associated with it, and similarly for the other spheres. This gives great freedom of movement while at the same time retaining a single idea. At later stages of the exercise, once the Middle Pillar itself is firmly established, the student may go on to use the appropriate colours for the various spheres, and to add the side pillars in their appropriate colours. These should preferably be taken from the astrological and chakra references which derive from AL rather than quasi-Hebrew systems.

9. Having mastered these phases of the technique, and fully accomplished the extension of the technique in time to the full period of three hours, or at the very least one and a half hours, the student may go on to perform rituals in the spheres. Whereas the meditation has been worked from top to bottom, the rituals must be worked from 'Malkuth' up. This entails a correspondence between the sections of the ritual(s) and the levels of the Middle Pillar (and only the Middle Pillar is to be employed). For the Pentagram Ritual and the 'Elemental' quarters of the Bornless Rite the correspondences are as follows: East = Malkuth. South = Yesod. West = Tiphereth. North = Da'ath. The student should not concern themselves at this point with the appropriateness or otherwise of these correspondences, but simply work with the rituals in these spheres, vibrating the various Names, and forming the various sigils, signs and lineal figures in the appropriate chakras. The *raison d'être* will become plain with practice. With the last two phases of the Bornless Rite the correspondences will be: Spirit Active = Ajna Chakra or 'third eye' (roughly 'Kether' as the cranial suture); Spirit Passive = Sahasrara Chakra or above the head (roughly Ain Soph or 'Kether' above the head). These equations are approximate, and as said above are not the practitioner's concern at this stage.

The preliminary phases of the ritual, such as the Purifications and Consecrations, should be worked in the Middle Pillar likewise. The Purifications consist of visualising a chalice above the head pouring water down, or alternatively a simple blue downwards-pointing equilateral triangle above the head, descending through the Middle Pillar. Whichever is employed, the water or triangle (or both, since both methods should be practised and may well coincide) descends to the heart chakra. The appropriate verse of *AL* is recited at the same time. The Consecrations are performed in a similar manner, so that the flame or red upright equilateral triangle ascends from the groin to the heart, where it interlocks with the water triangle. Again the appropriate verse from *AL* is recited internally. This exercise obviously will precede the Pentagram Ritual which in turn precedes the Bornless Rite.

10. If at any time in the course of performing these exercises the operator feels themselves tensing up or losing concentration then the entire process should commence anew, beginning with the tensing and relaxing phase. This tendency should be overcome before attempting to perform rituals in the Middle Pillar.

11. Once the student has acquired these abilities, they will find their accustomed magical procedures much enhanced, and may undertake these exercises without such great preparations. At this point in their career, they will be able to perform very sophisticated rituals in their Astral Body, whilst walking in the country or sitting in their armchairs. The effects of rituals performed in the physical body will also be greatly enhanced, to the point at which, for instance, other persons present, as in group rituals, will be aware of the changes in the Temple when they perform Banishing Rituals and so forth, and the effects of invocations will be enhanced to the point at which inducing states of possession in the Priestess will be a relatively minor matter. This is all in the future, however. The course of this initiation may well take some few years, despite the results of a six month preliminary retirement, which will be in themselves a substantial step forward. The reasons for this delay are difficult to establish. The most obvious reason is that the pressures induced by the operation set in motion the destruction of some major complexes and disorders in the student's make-up. The resolution of these takes some little time. This may be interpreted, rightly or wrongly, as a period of recovery from the Ordeal itself. It may also be seen as a period in which you rebuild your life after the obstacles in your environment, some of which may be extremely dear to you, have been removed.

The time at which the Ordeal and Retirement is undertaken should be astrologically determined, preferably coinciding with aspects for mystical achievement (Neptune/Pluto), and the period of resolution will of course depend on the transits and progressions of your natal chart. Difficulties encountered will almost certainly relate to the natal; the quality of results and their duration will also depend on astrological factors. Talented astrological magicians will find ways of off-setting some of these difficulties, and of lessening others, particularly once the Ordeal is over. The main stumbling block then is the degree to which your natal chart involves the possibility of this experience being available to you in the first place. The presence of bad aspects does not exclude the possibility of mystical and magical experience, but may well present difficulties. Such is the nature of Ordeals in any case. The presence of aspects involving such experiences is essential.

APPENDICES

Frequently Asked Questions

Why is the EQ Order & Value a serial order (one to twenty six) rather than hundreds, tens and units like the Hebrew system and others?

Many students of the Golden Dawn system and the better known sources on Greek and Hebrew Qabalah ask this question. In fact there is a considerable body of evidence that Greek and Hebrew characters were used for a serial order first, and that this order was important in the development of these systems. Similarly many other ritual alphabets have used serial orders rather than hundreds, tens and units. There is thus no reason why EQ should adhere to the same pattern as the systems which have had most currency since the nineteenth century. On the other hand the vast majority of alternative English Gematrias proposed since EQ's discovery have adopted the 1 to 26 'value' while proposing another 'order' for the letters.

Surely any attribution of numbers to letters would produce results? Isn't it more a matter of belief and 'word association by numbers'?

Apparently not, though before my own experience of EQ I might well have thought so myself. Several alternative gematrias do exist, but as yet none has produced a magical system. The question of belief is not appropriate to a true numerical system; numbers are a standard of immutable truth that rises above mythology and other limited paradigms. So far the alternative gematrias have indeed proved to be nothing more than systems of word association, or go little further than 'proving' the discoverer is Crowley's successor. EQ on the other hand has shown itself capable of considerably more than this, a situation that cannot be entirely due to the superior ability of its exponents!

The exception to this rule is the unpublished work on English gematria by David Allen Hulse. Though not extending to a magical methodology in itself, the system he uses is the simplest of all, the ABC series numbered 1 to 26, which the discoverers of the Elevenfold Qaballa had tried and not found of interest. My own researches also failed to find anything of interest in this schema.

Hulse on the other hand, and I take my hat off to him for it, came at the problem from another direction, as may be seen in his *Key of it All* which I cannot recommend too highly, and got first class results from what had seemed to some of the best qualified persons in this field to be an unlikely schema. Having surveyed and examined many alternative methods of English gematria it is my belief that more is to come, and that the serial order applied to ABC and its odd numbered permutations (of which 'family' EQ is an honoured member) is likely to be the most fertile area for future discoveries.

What simple proofs can you present that EQ is a valid solution to the Qabalistic puzzles of *The Book of the Law*?

Simple proofs are many, though in their enthusiasm EQ writers have often assumed the reader will find them for themselves and have concentrated on other more technical aspects. These following are among the simplest and most 'accessible' indicators of EQ's astonishing ability to detail Thelemic principles exactly without mind-bending calculation or peculiar spellings.

Many Thelemites are accustomed to writing 'Love is the law, love under will' as three 93's in reference to the Greek gematria values of Thelema and Agape. The value of LOVE IS THE LAW, LOVE UNDER WILL by EQ is 279 or 3x93. Similarly 'Do what thou wilt shall be the whole of the law' = 386 which is 2x193. The second chapter of *The Book of the Law*, states that the number of 'Had' is eleven, the value of HAD in EQ.

The phrase STRANGE DRUGS from *AL* has the value 143, the same value as the phrase DISTANT DRUG in *Liber VII*. This is a striking example of the accuracy of the gematria system, involving not only *AL* but the entire Class A literature.

The *Book of the Law* enjoins us to exceed by delicacy and drink by the eight and ninety rules of art. DELICACY = 98 by EQ; no other reason has ever been presented for the number of 'rules of art'.

The Thelemic Pentagram rituals frequently attribute Babalon to West and Water, while Aiwass/Aiwaz is frequently attributed to the direction of Air. BABALON = 65 = WATER, AIWAZ = 36 = AIR. Accordingly EQ-derived ritual corresponds closely with traditional ritual in this obvious respect and in others less obvious, without any necessity to squeeze round pegs into square holes by selective spelling or other contortions.

The Counting Well process detailed elsewhere in this book produces other startling proofs.

AZURE % LIDDED = 718 (Note eleven letters and the initials AL, the next word is 'Woman', thus the initials ALW, which are the first letters of the EQ Order & Value. Note also that the phrase 'O Azure-Lidded Woman' starts with the letters O.A.Z., which letters have the EQ values of 7.1.8.)

ABRAHAD % ABRA = 418 (Crowley's 'Hebrew' system gives the same value).

AUM % HA = 93 (this word seals the book).

SUN % MIDNIGHT = 666 (This number is traditionally associated with the Sun and with the 'Solar Phallic' current of which 'The Beast' is the embodiment. There are important keys in this equivalence, relating to Khephra, results magick and the IVth house of Astrology, the Enemy Naming Ceremony and much else.)

BABALON % BABALON = 910 (91 is a significant number, with or without considerations of the Hebrew system, since it is the sum of the numbers one to thirteen and the value of 13 x 7.

The EQ value of BABALON is 65, 65 + 91 = 156, the value of Babalon in Crowley's 'Hebrew' system.)

These simple proofs are outside the realm of coincidence and are unmatched by any alternative system. Neither Achad nor Crowley produced results of this quality or quantity with their Qabalistic analyses, simply because they lacked the tools. No alternative gematria schema has come close either. It is not a matter of 'my Qabalah is better than yours', though many responses to EQ have been based on such a petulant attitude. The 'English Qaballists' have done considerable research into all alternatives which have been put forward, and have often tried harder to extract sense from them than the proposers of the alternatives themselves. The vital thing to bear in mind is a Qabalah is a ritual language, and any proposed system that does not produce a magical system is not a Qabalah, whatever else it might be. I see no reason to reject the possibility of further numerical systems within *The Book of the Law*, but this is no argument against making use of the only one so far to produce practical results.

Ritual of the Pentagram

Begin in the centre of the circle, facing East. Formulate a brilliant sphere of light clearly above the head, radiant and powerful. Feel love and reverence for this sphere of light. Raise the right hand to it, then lowering it to the centre of the brow, say:

O GLORY BE;

dropping the hand to the genitals, say:

UNTO THEE;

retracing the line to the centre of the chest then touching the right shoulder, say:

THROUGH ALL TIME;

tracing back across the chest, touch the left shoulder and say:

AND THROUGH ALL SPACE.

Touching the centre of this Cross of Light, say again:

GLORY;

folding the arms one over the other in the position of Osiris Risen, say as the right hand rests on the left shoulder:

AND GLORY

and as the left crosses it and rests on the right shoulder:

UPON GLORY;

resting in this position conclude:

EVERLASTINGLY, AMEN & AMEN & AMEN.

Conclude with the Sign of Silence, imagining the godform to be of vast size and feeling the footstep of the god shaking the earth as you advance your foot.

Go anticlockwise to the East and draw the Banishing Pentagram of Earth, vibrating FIAT. Tracing the circle anticlockwise round to the South draw the Banishing Pentagram of Fire, vibrating APEP. Continue anticlockwise to the West, and draw the Banishing Pentagram of Water, vibrating BABALON; trace the line on anticlockwise to the North, draw the Banishing Pentagram of Air and vibrate AIWAZ. Complete the line back to the East and return to the centre, face East, spread your arms in the posture of Osiris Slain and say aloud, as if in the presence of powerful and benign gods:

BEFORE ME MATTER, BEHIND ME MOTION.
ON MY RIGHT HAND, TIME,
ON MY LEFT HAND, SPACE –
FOR ABOUT ME BLAZE THE PENTAGRAMS
AND IN THE COLUMN STANDS THE SIX
RAYED STAR.

This last line refers to an *AL* sigil above and below, which, while not consciously drawn, is implicit by virtue of your magical actions in this rite; they may therefore appear quite spontaneously, but if not they should be formulated clearly in the same way as the Pentagrams, but without being traced. In conclusion, repeat the Qaballistic Cross as in the beginning.

Another form of this ritual exists, using the Invoking Pentagrams of the Elements going clockwise but in the same order of directions and elements as above, the Pentagrams are charged first with the Highest Name of the force invoked then the Enochian sigil of the Element is drawn in the centre and charged with the Names given above, thus:

Earth Pentagram HOOR-APEP or ISIS-HATHOR,
Sigil FIAT.

Fire Pentagram NUIT, Sigil APEP.

Water Pentagram COPH NIA, Sigil BABALON.

Air Pentagram QADOSH-ISIS, Sigil AIWAZ.

Once the Circle has been completed in the East,
the ritualist faces WEST across the Altar in the Sign
of the Enterer (the posture of the central figure in 'The
Lovers' in the Thoth pack) and says aloud and with
intense solemnity and resonance:

THE WORDS AGAINST THE SON OF NIGHT,
TAHUTI SPEAKETH IN THE LIGHT.
KNOWLEDGE AND POWER, TWIN WARRIORS,
SHAKE
THE INVISIBLE, THEY ROLL ASUNDER THE
DARKNESS.
MATTER SHINES, A SNAKE.
SEBEK IS SMITTEN BY THE THUNDER.
THE LIGHT BREAKS FORTH FROM UNDER.

The palms of the hands must be directly above the
altar vertically, face down.

(The Magician who understands the nature of
the Ark, or of its counterparts, Dee's table and that
described in the Leyden papyrus, may make certain
additional gestures, blessing the altar after this part of
the ceremony with the appropriate signs, and the Name
RA HRUMACHIS = 113 = SPIRIT.)

The ritual then continues thus: go clockwise to
the West and face East, seeing the figure of the Hermit
in the Sign of the Enterer in the Eastern quarter just
vacated. Continue the ritual as above 'Before me

Matter...' etc. The Sigils, Pentagrams, fiery circle and
AL Sigils above and beneath must be maintained in the
mind's eye throughout. This ritual is much more potent
than the first, and may be used as a formal Temple
opening in EQ related work. On no account should it
be performed frivolously or without full knowledge of
the signs and symbols used; nor without full preparation,
robed and burning Abramelin or other holy perfume,
etc. Conclude as before with the Qaballistic Cross.

The rule to remember in the use of Pentagrams is
that in invoking, the Infinite Name is used to charge
the Pentagram and the Symbol Name to charge the
sigil, whereas in banishing, only the Symbol Name and
appropriate Pentagram is used. This is in accordance
with the tradition that in consecration the highest
symbol or Name of the force invoked is used, i.e. the
Infinite expression of the idea.

In Hexagram rituals, much the same rules apply.
Pentagrams are used to invoke the quarters and/or
elements, Hexagrams are used to invoke the planets, e.g.:
invoking Venus: draw Hexagram of Venus, vibrating the
Name from the Infinite scale, NUIT; draw sigil (either
the planetary sigil or the appropriate Enochian sigil)
vibrating the Name from the Symbol scale, IO PAN.
The Hymn to Pan may well be incorporated in the ritual
both for its use of the invokatory phrase IO PAN, and
for the effectiveness of this particular incantation in its
own right, which will be found to be appropriate to the
nature of many operations of Venus in any case.

It has not been found worthwhile to invoke the
signs as agencies. They serve rather the role of containers
and moderators of the planetary forces, and if they are

represented in the ritual it is in terms of Temple decor, and their influence will be as a modifier of the basic planetary energy. It is important to bear in mind with these tables that there can be no final version of the Names used. It appears to matter comparatively little, for example, in rituals of Jupiter, whether one uses ASAR + ISA for 48 or, equally valid numerically, LASTADZA, or even devises a new word, either by combining letters by addition to the required sum or taking a pre-existing word of the desired value and rearranging the letters to form a barbarous name.

This said, there are many cases in which the Names themselves impart information concerning the principle invoked. The yardstick of pure number in the use of invocations ensures that the practitioner will not stray from the path of truth, which might very easily occur in using names of various ancient cultures which are not fully understood. In the Tables of A.M.E.N. the mathematical relations between the planetary forces and the numbers are readily assimilated and will not serve you false. The importance of this is hard to over-emphasise, since these forces, which we gaily refer to as Planetary, are in fact only so on the mundane level (the fourth column, what Crowley would refer to as Mundane Chakras). On the higher levels they are little less than, and perhaps a good deal more than, divine forces.

We are dealing here with agencies akin to or identical with the 'Angelic' authors of the Enochian system or of AL itself. These forces are extremely potent; they are capable of initiating the magician by the most direct means, including drastic alterations in his or her mental, psychic and biochemical constitution.

An Invocation of Baphomet

Ritual 128.

I invoke Thee, Baphomet, Thou Union of Opposites in Infinity!
Thou art The Beast and Scarlet Woman conjoined!
Thou art Bes-na-Maut!
I see Thee in bright dew, thou that art the Fire & the Lamp!
Thou art the War-Engine of the Crowned Child – Thou Power of Life and Death!
Thou art the Five Wounds of the Ordeal X, the union of Sun and Venus!
Thou the Cube – Thou the Sacred Heart, bringing Lust & Worship into
Death!
By the Scarlet Woman and The Beast She rideth,
By the Lustral Wine & the Kisses of Nu...

In the Joy I behold Pan!
By the Lust & Worship!
By Life & Death,
& Fire & Lamp!

In the Joy of Thebes I charge you! Bringing the Force to my name!

The Force dwelleth in mine altars!

The Force dwelleth in!

Let us assume that a major ritual, involving several participants, is in progress. The temple is prepared, purified and consecrated, and various stages of the main ritual are already completed. It may be that some time has elapsed in this major celebration, that all preliminary stages are accomplished, especially the thorough integration of all present into a harmonious sodality, barriers down, enthused and working together. A further leap is required, not depending on any one celebrant but drawing on the power of all. This invocation is designed for just such a stage of a ritual. The main text is accompanied by a structure and further adorations and chants. With room for some adaptation once the ritual is understood, the following guidelines will produce incredible results.

The temple layout for this ritual resembles Crowley's Circle design having a central point, corresponding to his Tiphereth square, and three points of a large triangle, analogous to his 'triangle of yonis', compare with *Liber Pyramidos*, *Liber Yod*, *Liber 963* et al. Flanking the central point are two Priestesses, like the Kerubs on the Ark of the Covenant. At the three points of the triangle are the majority of the (male) initiates taking part, facing outwards and seated in a comfortable asana. The central point may be unoccupied or contain a talisman or chalice, or it may be occupied by a seated Priestess or a standing, masked priest.

Whatever the central focus consists of, the entire energy of the group is to be combined there, to be formed and directed by the Priestesses flanking it. Plenty of room is required, and the ritual may be best performed in a secluded outdoor location or a large chamber so no one has to sit facing a wall but has reasonable freedom of movement around them. There should be some light available, but not too much, and experienced ritualists will ensure that the light sets the atmosphere properly while avoiding fire hazards. With proper understanding every element of ritual may support this ecstatic state and direct it, while a clutter of paraphernalia will be a mere distraction.

The invocation given above may be declaimed by the most appropriate participant, such as a masked priest at the centre, a priestess assisting the Isis and Nepthys priestesses, a mobile *maître d'* or whomever. It should be passionately pronounced, and its seeming ambiguities made luminous by exaltation. All those seated at the three points of the triangle should visualise Baphomet behind them at the centre, having familiarised themselves with the selected image at an earlier date.

Whichever image of Baphomet is used, the hermaphroditic qualities should be prominent. Following the first and second verses one can insert barbarous names of invocation, such as a Wakanaba spell, the Names of the AMEN tables in the scale of 12 and so on, accompanied by the drawing of hexagrams and sigils appropriate to the rite.

It may well be that other priestesses are within the triangle performing a variety of tasks in support of the central pair, so that these can retain their positions and perform their tasks without distractions. These 'assistant priestesses' should endeavour to be unobtrusive. They may also take on any speaking roles that might otherwise be allotted to the main pair including the 'Song of the

Sirens', being their 'voice' as well as their 'hands' where necessary. From this it is to be inferred that the assistants are extensions of the two 'Goddesses', who also are one.

At the climax of this invocation the three points will 'divide' the name of Baphomet, the first point vibrantly pronouncing the first syllable, the second point the next syllable, naturally enough the last syllable is vibrated by the third point of the triangle, then the first point begins the cycle again. The Visualisation of Baphomet continues, appearing in the centre of the triangle behind them. It may be that a tingling in the spine accompanies the performance of this ritual.

Since the beginning of the chant the Isis and Nephthys priestesses have commenced another, the variously named 'Infernal Adorations of OAI' from *The Book of the Star Ruby*, also found in *The Vision and the Voice*. This chant in 'Moon language' may be replaced if desired, but if so the language used should be equally alien and appropriate to the task in hand. The divided name chant continues around the triangle while within it the priestesses sing the 'Song of the Sirens'. This is the beginning of their task at the centre. This task may be the consecration of a talisman or major sacrament, or a stage in an initiation or a prelude to possession (for a seated priestess between them). The precise nature of their task will determine what use they make of the energy raised and what appropriate actions are involved.

Conforming the visualised form of Baphomet to that of a priest or priestess occupying the centre may form part of the process. Whatever their precise task, the outside chant continues after the 'Song of the Sirens' is over and goes on through whatever task they undertake, and should build, becoming loud, inhuman and inspired around them. This is only concluded by a signal from the centre, such as a loud climactic Word or Words (brief, cutting through everything else – it is best if this 'Word' contains the entire ceremony and/or its purpose in Qabalistic form).

From here the ritual may be rounded off or proceed to another phase. If the ritual is to conclude, the celebrants of this invocation will most likely need 'bringing back down' gently after this stage, and the spiritual communality of the sacrament may be a good way of achieving this. On the other hand, the ritual may be taken on to another stage where the state induced will be taken further. This is left to the ingeniuum of the ritualists, but care should be taken as the psyches of the celebrants are not indestructible, and this is a powerful ritual, requiring some expertise and insight for its performance.

Finally, the following *Rite of Primal Heaven* is an incantation drawing on both the Stele and the Leyden Papyrus as well as the A.M.E.N. Tables. The text was composed for use with the Fifty Gates material detailed elsewhere in this book. The magician should develop and embellish this ritual in the light of their understanding, motivated by Aspiration to BABALON.

THE RITE OF PRIMAL HEAVEN

I

Open to Me O Heaven, Mother of the Gods!
So I shall see the Boat of Ra ascending and descending;
For I am Geb, Heir of the Gods,
making prayer before Ra My Father,
For that these things precede from Me.

O Hekau, Great One, Lady of the Shrine,
open to Me the Rishtret Gate,
Mistress of Spirits: Open to Me Primal Heaven;
let Me give honour to the Gods!
For I am Geb, true Heir of the Gods!

In the Name of the Great God F.I.A.T.;
Open to Me Primal Heaven!
In the Name of the Minister of the God, AIWAZ;
Open to Me Primal Heaven!
In the Name of the Scarlet Woman BABALON;
Open to Me Primal Heaven!
In the Name of the Fire Serpent APEP;
Open to Me Primal Heaven!
In the Name of the Lord of the Two Horizons,
RA-HRUMACHIS and of NEPTHYS, Sister of Isis:
Open to Me Primal Heaven!

My heart, My mother,
My heart, My mother,
My heart of My life upon Earth.
Do not witness against Me –
Before the Lord of the West;

Since I have united the Earth and Sky –
With the West while I lived upon Earth.

Hail! Ye Seven Kings! Ho! Ye Seven Spirits of Mentu!
He the Bull of Generation, Lord of Strength
That enlighteneth the Earth; Soul of the Void!
Ho Lion! Thou that art as the Lion of the Sky at Midday,
Thou who art as the Bull of the Sky before the morning;
Hail Thou that rulest the Kingdom of the East,
Great One, Lofty One!
Hail Soul of the Ram, Soul of the Kingdom of the West,
Hail Soul of Souls!
Great Bull of Heaven, Son of Nuit, Hail unto Thee!

In the Name of the Great God F.I.A.T.;
Open to Me Primal Heaven!
In the Name of the Virgin of Heaven, MARY;
Open to Me Primal Heaven!
In the Combined Name: NU-HAD;
Open to Me Primal Heaven!
In the Great Name IO PAN;
Open to Me Primal Heaven!
In the Name of Thy Minister, AIWAZ;
Open to Me Primal Heaven!
In the all powerful syllable AUM;
Open to Me Primal Heaven!
In the Name SOL INVICTUS;
Open to Me Primal Heaven!
In Thy Name of RA HOOR KHU;
Open to Me Primal Heaven!

Yea, in the Name of the Great God F.I.A.T.;
In the Name of the Twin Goddess, ASI-NEPTHI;
In the Name of the Great God HERU-RA-HA:
Open to Me for I am the Piercer of the Earth,
He that came forth from Geb!

II

I invoke the Great God, who giveth light exceedingly;
The Companion of the Flame;
In whose mouth is the Fire that is not quenched;
The Great God who is seated in the fire,
In the midst of the fire which is in the lake of heaven;
In whose hand is the sceptre of divine power:
Reveal Thyself to Me as to Thy Prophet!

PAN-IO-PAN!
Open to Me Primal Heaven.
By the Five Runes AOUIE!
Open to Me Primal Heaven.
O NUIT, Continuous One of Heaven!
Open to Me Primal Heaven.
AORMUZDI, Lord of Light!
Open to Me Primal Heaven.
Great TITAN of Sumer and Akkad!
Open to Me Primal Heaven.
ISIS, Queen of Starry Space!
Open to Me Primal Heaven.
Thou who art KHEPHRA at Midnight!
Open to Me Primal Heaven.
HADIT, burning in My heart!
Open to Me Primal Heaven.
By TAHUTI and the Child of the Prophet!
Open to Me Primal Heaven.
By Thy Minister AIWAZ!
Open to Me Primal Heaven.
In Thy tremendous Name MENTU!
Open to Me Primal Heaven.

III

O Great God, Who is above Heaven;
In whose hand is the beautiful staff,
Who created deity – deity not having created Him.
Who art seated upon the Mountain of Eternity;
Who dieth not – who liveth forever,
Open to Me Primal Heaven!

Yea in Thy Name of MENTU:
Open to Me Primal Heaven!
O MAUT, Vulture Goddess of the Twin Niles:
Open to Me Primal Heaven!
IACCHUS, Spirit of Ecstasy:
Open to Me Primal Heaven!
FALUTLI, FALUTLI! By the IOD and the PE:
Open to Me Primal Heaven!
By the Grand Word ABRAHADABRA
that is the Word of the Aeon:
Open to Me Primal Heaven!
O BES, COPH, KUT:
Open to Me Primal Heaven!
O Thou Twin God in One, HERU-RA-HA:
Open to Me Primal Heaven!
Great SET, the Terrible and Invisible God:
Open to Me Primal Heaven!
Great TYPHON, Thou Golden God!
Open to Me Primal Heaven!
By the Great God AL OAI and the word ABRA:
Open to Me Primal Heaven!
By the Great Combined Name NU-HAD-IT:
Open to Me Primal Heaven!

IV

O Thou God of Fire,
who art seated in the Invisible Darkness!
Thou Great God Who is in the midst of the
Company of Heaven!
Thou enthroned in Ra's Seat, Lord of the Aeon!
Open to Me Primal Heaven!

In the Name of the Prophet, ANKH AF NA KHONSU:
Open to Me Primal Heaven!
ISIS-HATHOR, HOOR-APEP,
Open to Me Primal Heaven!
QADOSH-ISIS:
Open to Me Primal Heaven!
By the Wand of the Force of COPH-NIA:
Open to Me Primal Heaven!
O Infinite Goddess NUIT:
Open to Me Primal Heaven!
By thine sacred Name of JESUS:
Open to Me Primal Heaven!
O Hawk-Headed God HERU:
Open to Me Primal Heaven!
By ASAR & ISA:
Open to Me Primal Heaven!
By Thy Threefold Book, O AIWASS, O YAMA:
Open to Me Primal Heaven!
By the ANKH, the Rose-Cross of Life and Light:
Open to Me Primal Heaven!
By Thine own, Thy Sovereign Name BAPHOMET:
Open to Me Primal Heaven!

Hail thou who art exalted,
Hail thou who art adored,
The Great One of Power,
The Divine Soul feared by the gods.
Thou who blazest upon Thy mighty throne.

Make a path for My soul,
For My spirit, for My shadow,
That I may shine forth as a divine living one
In the place of Ra and Tum, of Khephra and of Ahathoor.

O upraised arm of the shining Moon,
May I go forth among the multitudes,
And pass through the doors and dwell
Among ye in the region of stars;
That I may go forth as I please
Among those living upon Earth.

BIBLIOGRAPHY

This may be taken as a guide to further reading; however, it combines the functions of a reference of my sources, of some works which parallel themes in this book while not necessarily used in its preparation, some sources of opposite opinion which are no less significant for that, and a necessary recognition of influences underlying the ideas in the various chapters. Some source works differ in content from one edition to another, and in these cases I have given the most relevant edition. I have tried to give alternative titles for the non-Crowley works where I know of them. Since availability differs for many of these texts I have given titles rather than attempt to list the most recent publisher for a great many other works on this list. Ancient and Modern authors are not distinguished, however the works of some more recent authors are harder to obtain than any of the ancient ones referred to here. This attempt at bibliography is by no means exhaustive, the Indian sources in particular are inadequately covered, nor is it arranged in an orthodox manner, but hopefully the student will find it a useful guide to further study.

– JSK

Abraham the Jew. The Sacred Magic of Abramelin the Mage. Wellingborough, Northhamptonshire: Thorsons Publishers, Ltd., 1976.

Agrippa, Cornelius. Three Books of Occult Philosophy. St. Paul: Llewellyn, 1995. (Tyson's notes to the Llewellyn edition are extensive and valuable.)

Allegro, John. The Dead Sea Scrolls and the Christian Myth. Amherst: Prometheus Books, 1992.
---The Sacred Mushroom and the Cross. London: Hodder and Staughton, 1970.

Baigent, M., R. Leigh, and H. Lincoln. The Holy Blood and the Holy Grail. New York: Dell Publishing Co., 1983.

Bardon, Franz. The Key to the True Quabbalah. Wuppertal, West Germany: Deiter Ruggenberg, 1975.

Barrett, Francis. The Magus. Secausus: University Books, 1975.

Barry, Kieren. A Brief History of Gematria, Supplement to 1989 edition of Liber MCCLXIV. Privately published by the O.T.O. (Excellent.)

Bertiaux, Michael. The Voudun-Gnostic Workbook. New York: Magickal Childe, 1988. (Extremely solipsist, but has merit as modern 'Practical Qabalah'.)

Blavatsky, Helena Petrovna. The Secret Doctrine. Pasadena: Theosophical University Press, 1970.

Bonner, John. Qabalah: A Primer. London: Skoob Books Publishing, Ltd., 1995.

Brewster, Charles. Liber Cyber. London: BM Dazzle, 1991. (Among other gems this privately published work deals with 'astrological ritual timing' from the perspective of an experienced Chaos magician trained in astro-physics!)

Budge, E.A.Wallace. Amulets and Talismans. New Hyde Park: University Books, 1961.
---Gods of the Egyptians. New York, Dover, 1969.
---The Egyptian Book of the Dead. London: Routledge and Kegan Paul Ltd., 1974.

Carroll, Pete. Liber Null. York Beach: Samuel Weiser, Inc., 1987.
---Liber Kaos. York Beach: Samuel Weiser, Inc., 1992. (Highly recommended source books for magical techniques of all kinds.)

Carus, Paul. Chinese Occultism. (Also known as Chinese Astrology.) La Salle: Open Court, 1974.

Cleator, P.E. Lost Languages. London, Robert Hale & Co., 1959.

Crowley, Aleister. The Book of the Law. (This Book is utterly essential to the system described in this work, Liber 187.)
---The Book of Thoth. New York: Samuel Weiser, Inc., 1972.
---The Confessions of Aleister Crowley. London & New York: Penguin/Arkana, 1989.
---The Equinox, Volume 1. York Beach: Samuel Weiser, Inc., 1992. (Limited edition of 750 copies.)
---The Equinox, Volume III. York Beach: Samuel Weiser, Inc., 1992. (Limited edition of 1000 copies.)
---The Holy Books of Thelema. York Beach: Samuel Weiser, Inc., 1989.
---Little Essays Towards Truth. Scottsdale: New Falcon Publications, 1991.
---Magical Record of the Beast 666. London: Duckworth, 1972.

    The following references by Crowley are also contained in various editions, many included in the books above.

Liber O.
Liber Oz.
The Vision and the Voice.
Liber ABA. otherwise known as Magick. O.T.O. revised and enlarged edition. 1994.
The Equinox of the Gods. (Contained in above.)
The Psychology of Hashish.
Liber MCCLXIV.
Liber D.
Liber 777.
Liber Samekh.
Liber Resh.
Liber E.
Liber Ru.
Liber Astarte.
Liber HHH.
John St. John.
Introduction to Levi's Key of the Mysteries.

Liber Pyramidos.
Liber 231.
Liber Israfel.
Hail Mary. Also known as 'Amphora'.
De Arte Magica.
De Natura Deorum.
De Nuptiis Secretis Deorum cum Hominibus.
Agape (vel Liber C vel Azoth).
De Homonculo Epistola.
Two Fragments of Ritual.
Liber B vel Magi.

King, Francis, ed. The Gospel According to George Bernard Shaw.
(Edited by Francis King as Crowley on Christ).
---Astral Projection, Magic and Alchemy. Rochester: Destiny
Books, 1991.
---Ritual Magic in England. London: Neville Spearman, 1970.
---Secret Rituals of the O.T.O. London: C.W. Daniel, 1973.
(Contains many of the Crowley works with Latin titles given above.)

Cutner, H. A Short History of Sex Worship. London: Watts and Co.,
1940. (Foreword by Maurice Canney, Emeritus Professor of Semitic
Languages and Literatures in the University of Manchester, etc.).

Daraul, Arkon. Secret Societies, Yesterday and Today. London, F.
Muller, 1961.

Dee, John (Doctor). Spiritual Diaries. London: British Library,
Sloane MS. 3188.
---Heptarchia Mystica. London: British Library, Sloane MS. 3191.
---Monas Hieroglyphica. London: British Library, reference number
unknown.

Dunne, J.W. An Experiment with Time. New York: Macmillan,
1981. (Highly recommended, hugely influential work.)

Ebertin, Rheinhold, The Combination of Stellar Influences.
American Federation of Astrologers, 1972. (Ebertin nearly
singlehandedly revolutionised astrological thinking; this, possibly
his greatest book, provides interpretative tables of startling accuracy
as well as his groundbreaking 'Midpoint' technique.)

Eco, Umberto. The Search for the Perfect Language. Wiley-
Blackwell, 1997

Farr, Florence. Egyptian Magic. London: Aquarian Press, 1982.

Fortune, Dion. The Mystical Qabalah. York Beach: Weiser, 1984. (Often overestimated but still a classic work.)

Fuller, J.F.C. (Major General). Liber 963: The Treasure House of Images. (Highly recommended.)

Gibbon, Edward. The Decline and Fall of the Roman Empire. London: Methuen, 1909-14.

Ginsburg, Christian D. The Kabbalah, Its Doctrines, Development, and Literature. London: George Routledge & Sons, 1925. (Recommended, it is far superior to Mathers' Kabbalah Unveiled, which is only good insofar as it plagiarises Ginsburg.)

Grant, Kenneth. The Magical Revival. London: Frederick Muller, Ltd., 1972.
---Aleister Crowley and the Hidden God. London: Frederick Muller, Ltd., 1973.
---Cults of the Shadow. New York: Sameul Weiser, Inc., 1976.
---Nightside of Eden. London: Frederick Muller, Ltd., 1977.
---Remembering Aleister Crowley. London: Skoob   Books Publishing, Ltd., 1991.

Graves, Robert. The White Goddess. New York: Noonday Press, 1997. (Excellent book on alphabet mysticism and much more besides.)

Gray, William. Magical Ritual Methods. New York: Samuel Weiser, Inc., 1980.
---The Rite of Light. Privately printed, 1976.
---Outlook on our Inner Western Way. New York: Samuel Weiser, Inc., 1980.
---A Self Made by Magic.
---Inner Traditions of Magic. New York: Samuel Weiser, Inc., 1970.

Greene, Deirdre. Gold in the Crucible. Dorset: Element Books Ltd., 1989.

Heidrick, Bill. O.T.O. Newsletter. Ordo Templi Orientis, Spring, 1978. (The author's kabbalistic writings are all worthy of attention.)

Hulse, David Allen. The Key of it All. St. Paul: Llewellyn Publications, 1995. (Highly recommended compendium of alpha-numeric systems.)

Huson, Paul. Mastering Witchcraft. New York, Berkley Publishing Group, 1980. (The first 'hands on' book that I read–and used. Highly recommended. Complete with an excellent bibliography.)
---The Devils Picturebook. New York: Putnam Press, 1971. (Tarot is the theme but Huson delivers an insightful account of magical theory and practice in the process; a true 'radical traditionalist'.)

Hutchinson's Encyclopedia. London: Guild Publishing, 1988.

Iraneus of Lugdunum. Against the Heresies. Lincoln: The Society for Promoting Christian Knowledge, year unknown.

Jones, Charles Stansfield (Frater Achad). Liber 31. San Francisco: Level Press, 1974.
---QBL, The Brides Reception. New York: Samuel Weiser, Inc., 1969.
---Stepping Out of the Old Aeon into the New. (Often wrongly attributed to Aleister Crowley).

Josephus. History and Antiquities of the Jews. Trans. by William Whiston. Grand Rapids: Kregel Publications, 1999.

Jung, Carl. Four Archetypes. London: Routledge and Kegan Paul, 1972.
---Man and his Symbols. London: Aldus Books, 1964.
---Secret of the Golden Flower. (Commentary). Trans. by CF Byanes. London: Routledge & Kegan Paul, 1968.

Kaplan, Aryeh. Meditation and the Kabbalah. Northvale: Jason Aronson, 1998.
---Meditation and the Bible. York Beach: Samuel Weiser: 1988.
---The Bahir. York Beach: Samuel Weiser: 1990.
(The first title here is particularly informative, covering ground Mathers, AC, et al never touched on.)

Kersten, Holger. Jesus Lived in India. Dorset: Element Books, 1994.

King, C.W. The Gnostics and their Remains. Kila: Kessinger Publishing Co., 1942. Facsimile edition.

Kuhn, Alvin Boyd. Esoteric Structure of the Alphabet. Kila: Kessinger Publishing Co., 1997. ('A study on the esoteric meaning of the English alphabet in the light of Hebrew and Sanskrit symbolism.')

Langford, Trevor. Astrology Articles in The Equinox: British Journal of Thelema, Volume 7, Dorset: Kiblah Publishing, 1992.
Lea, S. & Bond, B. The Apostolic Gnosis. Kila: Kessinger Publishing Co., 1942. Facsimile edition.
---Gematria. London: Research Lost Knowledge, 1977.

Lees, James. The New Equinox, Volume 5 and 6, Dorset: Kiblah Publishing, 1992.
---The Qaballa of AL. Tamworth: private printing, 1982. (The fountainhead of English Qaballa.)

Lempriere, J. Lempriere's Classical Dictionary. London: Routledge & Kegan Paul, 1949 .

The Leyden Papyrus: An Egyptian Magical Book. New York: Dover 1974.

Levi, Eliphas. Transcendental Magic. New York: Samuel Weiser, Inc., 1968.
---Psuedo-Magriti: The Picatrix. (Properly called The Aim of the Sage.) London: The Warburg Institute, University of London, 1962.

Magee, Michael. The Sri Yantra and Sidereal Astrology. Oxford: Mandrake. Privately printed.
---Tantric Astrology. (Revised and enlarged version of above.) Oxford: Mandrake, 1989.
(Mike is the former editor of the much respected magazine Sothis, his Website is a very valuable resource.)

Massey, Gerald. Ancient Egypt, the Light of the World. New York: Samuel Weiser, Inc., 1973.
---A Book of the Beginnings. Secausus: University Books, Inc., 1974.
---The Natural Genesis. New York: Samuel Weiser, Inc., 1974.
(Influential and criminally neglected author.)

Mathers, S. L. The Kabbalah Unveiled. London & New York: Penguin/Arkana, 1991. (Get Ginsburg's book instead!)

Mead. G.R.S. Thrice Greatest Hermes. Kila: Kessinger Publishing Co., 1997. (Valuable compendium of Hermetic literature, it includes a Naasene text dealing with sexual gnosis.)

Michell, John. The Dimensions of Paradise. London: Thames and Hudson, 1988.

Monod, Jacques. Chance and Necessity: An Essay on the Natural Philosophy of Modern Biology. New York, Knopf, 1971. (Highly recommended.)

Orpheus, Rodney. Abrahadabra. Stockholm: Looking Glass Press, 1995.

Parsons, Jack. The Book of Babalon.

Peake, A.S. A Commentary on the Bible. London: Thomas Nelson Publishers, 1952. (Old collection of scholarly essays on biblical history, customs, influences and so on.)

Regardie, Israel. The Complete Golden Dawn System of Magic. Tempe, New Falcon Publication, 1990.
---A Garden of Pomegranates. St Paul: Llewellyn Publications, 1999.
---Secret Inner Order Rituals of the Golden Dawn. Tempe, New Falcon Publications, 1996.
---Gems from the Equinox. Tempe, New Falcon Publications, 1982. (Contains many of the Crowley works referenced above.)
---The Middle Pillar. St. Paul, Llewellyn Publications, 1998. (Very important work, the technique has applications throughout magical work.)
---Ceremonial Magick. St. Paul, Llewellyn Publiations, 1989. (Contains Greek text of the Bornless Rite.)

Runciman, Steven. The Medieval Manichee. Cambridge: Cambridge University Press, 1983.

Scholem, Gershom G. Major Trends in Jewish Mysticism. Hoborn: Thames and Hudson, 1955.
---On the Kabbalah and its Symbolism. New York: Schocken, 1969.
---Origins of the Kaballah. Princeton: Princeton, 1987.

Spare, Austin Osman. The Book of Pleasure. Private printing.
---Focus of Life. Private printing.
---Axiomata and the Witches Sabbath. Private printing.
(Spare has been claimed as an Ancestor of Chaos Magic, but there are many senses in which Spare can be acclaimed as the Ancestor of modern Practical Qaballa.)

Stirling, William. The Canon: An Exposition of the Pagan Mystery perpetuated in the Caballa as the Rule of all the Arts. London: Garnstone Press, 1974.

Stratton-Kent, Jake. The Equinox: British Journal of Thelema, Volume 7, Issues 1-8, Dorset: Kiblah Publishing, 1992.
---The Equinox: British Journal of Thelema, Volume 7, Issues 9-11, Wakefield: Hadean Press, 2010.
---The Book of the Law and its Qaballa. Dorset: Kiblah Publishing, 1994.

Swete, H.B. The Apocalypse of St. John. London: MacMillan, 1906.

Symonds, John. The Great Beast. London: Granada Publishing, Ltd., 1973.

Thompson, Cath. L. Tamworth: Kaaba Publications, 1995.
(Contains a valuable and important introductory essay.)

U.D., Frater. Practical Sigil Magic. St. Paul: Llewellyn, 1990.

Wilson, Steve. Chaos Ritual. London: Neptune Press, 1994.

Yates, Frances A. (Dame). Giordano Bruno and the Hermetic Tradition. London: Routledge and Kegan Paul, 1964.

Zumm, Sophie. 'Every Woman is a Star'. The Equinox: British Journal of Thelema. Vol. 7, Issue 5. Dorset: Kiblah Publishing, 1992.

Glossary

Astrology (Astro-Qaballa): Ritual language and symbolic structure based on the exterior order of the heavens and various analogies with the human body. Almost every major tradition of antiquity can be understood only by reference to astrology. The esoteric sense of the astrological symbolism is of far greater significance than the 'divinatory' applications. Ritual timing need not presuppose a causal relation between planetary movements and terrestrial events.

Caballa: Generally denotes the Renaissance adaptation of the Hebrew system; the 'Christian Caballa' of Mirandola and Agrippa.

Chaos Magick: An important modern occult school emphasising magical technique and influenced strongly by Crowley and Spare. Not to be omitted by students seeking 'living' schools in which to acquire and hone their skills.

Cult:

a) Religious grouping and their methodology.

b) The elements of magick which involve devotional methods common to Ceremonial Magick, Tantra and Bhakti Yoga. Also the use of particular personifications of archetypes for magical or mystical purposes. The use of prayer and formulae in such activities as consecrating the instruments and materials for a given ritual are examples of cultic methodology. The existence of a coherent and flexible archetypal symbolism in an occult tradition, whereby such cult elements may be usefully retained and a personal ritual language developed should be welcomed. It would be unwise to abandon scepticism and critical appraisal in favour of crude 'faith' in such symbols and personifications, but it is equally unwise to consider these elements unhelpful or indicative of dogmatism. See *syncretism*.

Enochian: The magical system of John Dee, intended to supersede the Hebrew system.

Gematria: The method of converting words into numbers by number-letter equivalence. In modern use this term is borrowed from the Hebrews, who borrowed it from the Greeks. The method is far older than the Kabbalah and there is no good reason to suppose it originated in connection with the Hebrew language. The term *alphanumerics* is a reasonable modern equivalent without inferred cultural bias.

Gnosticism: A religious tradition advocating Gnosis (or spiritual knowledge) as superior to Faith, a major opponent of early Christianity, of which it is the true form.

Grimoire Tradition: The medieval grimoires are ceremonial manuals with a strong emphasis on invocation and evocation. The methods include elaborate ceremonies and prayer alongside fasting, sleep deprivation, periods of celibacy and so on. The use of religious ceremonies may be ascribed to superstition, deliberate blasphemy or whatever one pleases; essentially however it forms an important element of the technique regardless of how we may choose to analyse its use outside of the grimoires' real context. Strongly influenced by Kabbalah and Gnosticism.

Kabbalah: The Hebrew system of alpha-numeric mysticism which deeply influenced Western occultism from the Middle Ages up to the nineteenth century 'Occult Revival'. Not identical to earlier forms of Jewish mysticism which have often been confused with it, Kabbalah represents a reinfusion of Gnostic and Neoplatonist ideas into European culture.

Magick: Occult means of participation in the processes of change and chance. A combination of psycho-spiritual techniques and the manipulation of consciousness through symbols. An experiential and individualistic system, the combination of Sceptical and Cultic elements is essential if seemingly paradoxical. Attempts to accommodate Magick to a Scientific (parapsychological) or Religious (miraculous) perspective are only effective as camouflage or propaganda.

Mantra: A tantric term indicating a verbal or mental chant devised according to the alphabetical symbolism of the Sanskrit language. By extension any phrase or word repeated as a concentration aid or for magical purposes. Alpha-numerical ideas are frequently associated with Sanskrit and other mantras.

Merkabah: Literally 'Chariot', a major system of Jewish Gnosticism, with an established connection to the prophetic tradition. Linear descent from this tradition to the medieval Kabbalah is sustainable only as a myth or metaphor, however they have elements in common despite this difficulty.

Qabalah:

a) Denotes the nineteenth century Hermetic revision of the Christian Cabala. Insofar as it has no relation to any sacred text, it is to a large extent not a Cabala at all but a complex system of correspondences relying on obsolete religious forms.

b) A generic term with no necessary link to the Hebrew system, representing instead the use of an alpha-numeric cosmological model to generate a ritual language.

Qaballa: This spelling ALWAYS refers to the English Qaballa; the spelling, structure and gematria of the word are not arbitrary but deliberate. It has been objected by traditionalists that, with no specifically Hebraic content, English Qaballa should go under a different name. However, since the Hermetic Qabalah is so far distinct from the Hebrew Kabbalah as to render the retention of the Hebrew elements anachronistic or at least unnecessary, such objections tend to rebound on their authors.

Syncretism: Syncretism endeavours to unify or reconcile differing religious and mystical systems. Gnosticism and Neo-Platonism were notable syncretic movements paralleled in more recent times by Theosophy; similarly 'The Golden Dawn synthesis' and Crowley's extension of it are syncretist. The true unity is not in ideology but in method. There is thus no necessary incompatibility between the so-called 'pragmatic' and 'dogmatic' (sic) schools of modern magick.

Tantra:

a) System of attainment involving sexual technique, alphabet mysticism (mantra) and astrological symbolism. 'The Qabalah of the Indians'.

b) A book of this tradition is called a Tantra.

Taoism: Important Chinese school of mysticism and magick. Medieval and Renaissance ideas of Alchemy were strongly influenced by Taoism, and there are striking parallels between this ancient philosophy and the ideas of Crowley and Spare. Taoism as a broad tradition rather than a philosophy and contains elements of shamanism, sexual magic, complex ceremonial, divination, astrology and alchemy. There are striking correspondences between Taoist occultism and certain elements of 'Qabalah'. A prime example is in the structure of the Yi King, which derives from the linear symbols of the Yin and Yang (2 lines), which are first combined into four double combinations (8 lines), and thence into eight 'trigram' combinations (24 lines) and from thence to 64 'hexagram' combinations (384 lines). 2+8+24+384=418. Still more striking is the similarity between the diagram of the 'Supreme Pole' and the Kabbalistic Tree of Life.

Thelema: The most important modern school of occultism originating with Aleister Crowley; as a forward looking 'synthesis' it exceeds the Golden Dawn in scope and its sceptical methodology is paralleled rather than improved on by the more recent Chaos Magick.

Yantra: Cosmological diagram or symbol of the Tantric tradition. The most important is the Sri Yantra, as significant to that tradition as the Tree of Life is to the Qabalah.

ABOUT THE AUTHOR

JAKE STRATTON-KENT BEGAN PRACTICING MAGICK IN 1972, convinced that hands-on involvement should be part of the learning experience from day one. Between performing arduous Solomonic rites and casting spells of Eclectic Witchcraft, he set himself the task of devouring the serious literature of occultism, past and present. So successful was he in this task that he was soon made advisor on occult literature to a specialist bookstore in the home town of Aleister Crowley.

He took a lifelong Vow of Service to Isis in 1974, a significant act considering his strong opposition to the now declining Phallocentric emphasis in Thelemic magick. He took the Oath of a Probationer to A∴ A∴ in 1976, without the benefit of a Mentor. He undertook the task of performing the curriculum of A∴A∴ in the Outer. This task he completed largely without supervision by 1982. Around this time he became a contributor to occult magazines, and renewed his acquaintance with the pioneers of Chaos Magic whom he had met by chance in the mid-1970s. When Ray Sherwin decided to hand on the journal *The New Equinox*, Jake was the first to be offered the job of editor, but instead became a regular contributor under its second editorial team. This Thelemic magazine had been the original launching pad for Chaos Magick, and in its new guise provided the first public revelations regarding the English Qaballa.

Through this valuable association, Jake's A∴A∴ work took a new turn with an Abramelin style retirement. In 1984 he unexpectedly inherited Outer responsibility for an A∴A∴ aligned Magical Order, and in 1988 *The New Equinox* entered its third phase of existence under his editorship. Fourteen years after the publication of Issue 8 of *The Equinox: British Journal of Thelema*, Hadean Press took up the torch to continue this most necessary volume, with Jake at the helm. 2009 saw the release of Jake's book, *The True Grimoire*, a major contribution to the practice and study of goetic magic. This was followed in 2010 by *Geosophia*, a two volume work tracing the development of the Western grimoiric tradition.

With these roles and publications have come many opportunities for lecturing. Ever the campaigner, Jake's informal and enthusiastic style continues to bring previously neglected or specialized areas of occultism into the vanguard of contemporary magick.

A balance of traditional methods and modern innovation has been a major feature throughout his occult career. His involvement in the eclectic paths of modern Witchcraft and Chaos Magic has been balanced by a healthy respect for the strand of astrological magick from ancient times to Cornelius Agrippa and onwards. His impartial attitude and rare ability to combine ancient and modern approaches have made him a controversial and respected figure in contemporary occultism.

CPSIA information can be obtained at www.ICGtesting.com
Printed in the USA
LVOW10s1931150614

390137LV00025B/649/P

9 781907 881077